THE DENVER POST

Guide to the Best Family Films

52 Great Movies to Fill Up Your Year

Michael Booth

Johnson Books
Boulder

To my wife, Pam,
and my kids, Maya, Madeline, and Quinn,
who make movie nights so much fun.

Published by Johnson Books, a Big Earth Publishing company, 3005 Center Green Drive, Suite 220, Boulder, Colorado 80301. E-mail: books@bigearthpublishing.com www.bigearthpublishing.com 1-800-258-5830

Cover design by Jekaterina Girtakovska
Text design and layout by cbgraphics, Constance Bollen

9   8   7   6   5   4   3   2   1

Library of Congress Cataloging-in-Publication Data on file

Printed in the United States of America

Contents

On the Couch

My first family movie memory: *The Computer Wore Tennis Shoes* is on TV at one end of our crowded living room in Northern California. I believe I'm about six years old.

Dexter Reilly (Kurt Russell) and Dean Higgins (Joe Flynn) are having another bickering session about proper behavior at legendary Medfield College, and my two brothers and two sisters and I are having another bickering session about who gets to sit where. Sunday night's *Wonderful World of Disney* was a ritual at our house, and so was the seating arrangement: If you wanted ice cream from the kitchen, you could preserve your spot in the favored green chair or black chair, but only if you said "Saves on the green chair!" or "Saves on the black chair!" loud enough to be heard over Kurt Russell—or over my sister's junior high phone conversations. "If you forgot to call 'Saves!' then when you returned from the kitchen you'd face a wrestling match with your trespassing older brother."

Fast-forward six years. I'm about twelve. My parents take me to a small-town northern Minnesota movie theater playing *Saturday Night Fever*. It's rated R, but there I am, squirming in my chair as Tony Manero, John Travolta's character, has an unpleasant sex scene with the Brooklyn tramp played by Donna Pescow. Driving home, my parents are mortified that they didn't check the movie out first to protect their previously clueless, now bug-eyed youngest son. My mom turns to me in the back seat, and says, "You know, Mike, when a man and a woman are together, it's not always like that. It's much more beautiful."

Fast forward to age forty. Grandma and Grandpa, their five children, the children's spouses, and thirteen grandchildren and cousins are crowded into a small living room at a lake house to watch *Return of the Pink Panther*. The hilarity of Peter Sellers's comic performance as Inspector Clouseau crosses all generations, genders, and sensibilities. Grandparents are snickering, parents are giggling, eight-year-olds are cackling. When Sellers sucks the canary into the vacuum cleaner, pandemonium breaks out.

Those are just some of my movie memories, some of the pleasures that movies have brought to my life. I hope you'll make your own memorable scenes over a lifetime of family movie nights, with a little help from this book. In a world where everyone has a private iPod, cable channels locked into TiVo, and an X-Box for every room in the house, watching a movie together remains the best family night in town. A good movie is an engrossing, shared experience that can lead to revelation, understanding, argument, and, most simply, entertainment. The right movie is something to be enjoyed by everyone in the family.

The movie discussions on the following pages first appeared in *The Denver Post* in my Tuesday family movie column. I've put fifty-two headlining movies together here to give your family a film gem every week for a full year. I mention other movies along the way, so that you can explore choices for years to come, too.

So what makes for a great family movie?

Page through these choices, and you'll find films as diverse as the science- and personality-rich entertainment *Contact*, aimed squarely at adults, and the adolescent silliness of *Meatballs*, aimed squarely at anyone but adults—but sure to please them, too. You'll find foreign films you've never heard of, like the vibrant and emotionally wrenching *The Color of Paradise*, and simplistic, lilting cartoon fare like *The Little Bear Movie*—the last of which is aimed squarely at four-year-olds.

What binds them together is that first of all, of course, I love them. More important, they've earned the love of families, too, from 1972 to just last night. Many movies are merely "good" or "good enough"—like *Spider-Man*, or *Simon Birch*, or *The Sponge Bob Squarepants Movie*. The world won't end if you don't see them. The films chosen here earned their place when somewhere in the world, a mom asked another mom, say, "What movie should we rent tonight?" and the answer she got was a tight grip on the arm, an intense stare into the eyes, and the heated advice, "You have got to see *Sounder*. Your kids won't believe how they treated poor people back then."

Or, "We loved *Searching for Bobby Fischer*. It's about this kid who plays chess, and he hangs out with some strange people, and his dad is a little intense."

Or, "If you're not crying by the end of *October Sky*, I don't want to be your friend anymore."

These movies have fans, not just people who watched them. Sometimes, I may be the only fan—to appreciate *The Little Bear Movie* fully, for instance, it helped to be bleary-eyed at 1:00 in the morning, with a two-year-old on my shoulder suffering from a double ear infection, when three hours of crying suddenly ceased because there was a funny little bear sitting on his father's shoulders and Shawn Colvin singing a beautiful song.

Most people don't think of *Butch Cassidy and the Sundance Kid* for family viewing, but who better to appreciate blowing up a boxcar full of dollar bills or an outlaw being kicked in the sensitive regions than your eight-year-old boy? And who else besides me is going to remind you to go back twenty-seven years for *My Bodyguard*, so that your adolescents can understand that the horrors of middle and high school are a timeless, universal experience?

There are DVDs here your family might not finish. *The Gods Must Be Crazy* is an acquired taste. *I'm Not Scared* may seem too intense for your younger children, not to mention the subtitles problem. There may not be enough hankies in the house to get all of you through *The Champ*.

No worries. Family movie night is never perfectly smooth, anyway. Somebody scratches the DVD. The neighbors stop by for a trip to the ice cream store. The dog throws up popcorn. These movies are suggestions, not mandates. And when things go wrong at the movies, the family may still wind up with a happy ending. My mom might have kicked herself for taking me to see *Saturday Night Fever* before my time, but I'll never forget what she said afterward, and the feeling that a movie could be the beginning of a lifelong conversation with my parents.

I want you to become a fan of the movies, but we don't have to rave about the same things. If you see the listing for *Time Bandits* and would rather watch *The Adventures of Baron Munchausen* instead, be my guest. If Dad sees the car chases in *The Italian Job* and decides to rent *Ronin* or *The Bourne Identity* next time, all the better. If mom can't get over how cute Tom Hanks looks in *Big*, yes, yuck, but good for her.

Every spot on the couch gives us a slightly different angle on a movie. The important thing is that, for a few moments at least, we were all arguing about the same pictures.

Taking the "Arrr!!!" out of "Rated R"

Seabiscuit is a nostalgic, sepia-toned family movie about hope and perseverance.

Hotel Rwanda is a violent, disturbing, depressing account of the horrifying tribal genocide in central Africa that murdered hundreds of thousands of people. I'd happily watch *Seabiscuit* with an eight-year-old. I'd think twice before showing *Hotel Rwanda* to the average fifteen-year-old.

Both films got a PG-13 rating from the Hollywood review board.

Most recently came the news that smoking in a movie, even by adults of legal age, could push a film into a more restricted ratings category. Bugs Bunny, stub out that stogie, or the kids may never see the classic "A Wild Hare" again! Zealous raters might slap a warning of "pervasive smoking" on the Oscar-nominated *Good Night, and Good Luck*, thus scaring off school systems who might otherwise let their teenagers see a fascinating movie about McCarthyism and the First Amendment.

The current ratings system drives most parents nuts, sooner or later. With good reason. An oversexed, teen-bimbo, anti-female movie like *Mean Girls* gets away with PG-13, and yet the touching coming-of-age story *Stand by Me* gets an R because—surprise!—teenage boys tend to swear.

Yet there are two constants, and one new fact, about the ratings system that should all come as consolation to parents picking a film for movie night.

First, the current ratings have proven surprisingly adaptable to changing mores since the PG-13 designation was added in 1984. The private ratings board, though shrouded in unnecessary secrecy, has frequently changed its rulings in a useful system of protests and editing requests from filmmakers. Second, the current private and voluntary ratings system is better than the most likely alternative: an official government censor. Do you really trust changing presidential administrations or local vice boards to decide what movies are "appropriate" for which age groups? As a parent who has lived through the taste-making eras of Edwin Meese, Tipper Gore, and Alberto Gonzales, I know that things could be far worse.

Finally, that new fact: the Internet has made it easy for parents to get detailed information about sex, violence, profanity, drug use, and other potentially offensive topics concerning every movie ever produced. Family movie night no longer has to be an awkward gamble, wondering if Grandma will blanche at an F-bomb, or whether a ten-year-old will have to sit through a too-graphic love scene. If the PG-13 rating tells you almost nothing, don't give up: busy factotums at websites from Sceneit.com to Pluggedinonline.com are happy to tell you exactly how much sexual innuendo resides in *Big*.

Some websites cull their movies through a religious filter, others on questions of taste or age levels. You'll find the tone you are most comfortable with, and then you can bookmark that page for future use. You can always e-mail me at mbooth@denverpost.com if you want my take on an appropriate family night movie. My memory is a leaky colander at best, but I know where to look to get the answers.

Here are a few of the websites you will find most useful in screening movie choices for your family nights:

• Screenit (www.screenit.com) is a nonjudgmental site offering two levels of service: Free reviews accompanied by a lot of ads, and a subscription level to skip ads and receive all the latest reviews. Screenit's back catalog of reviews grows deeper by the month, and parents will find the detailed descriptions extremely helpful in logical areas of concern: "guns / weapons," "imitative behavior," and the like.

• www.pluggedinonline.com is the media-criticism arm of the Christian fundamentalist group Focus on the Family. You may disagree with the group's social and political opinions, but the surprisingly open-minded reviews here are well written and useful. They add categories such as "spiritual content" to their descriptions, and they come down harder on many popular movies than other review sites.

• Parent Previews (www.parentpreviews.com) does not boast the massive back catalog you might need to check on more obscure titles, but it does feature articulate and detailed reviews by true fans of film. A good resource for new releases in theaters, its appeal is sometimes marred by massive advertising sponsorships.

- The motto of www.familymediaguide.com is, "We provide the details, you decide." This neutral site is a wealth of good information, and it also provides family-friendly screenings of video games, TV shows, and other media.

- For an unabashedly religious filter on the media your children are exposed to, try www.movieguide.org. The website is "dedicated to redeeming the values of the mass media according to biblical principles by influencing entertainment industry executives and helping families make wise media choices." Forewarned, you can browse through their hearty endorsements of mediocre fare like *Firehouse Dog*.

- I appreciate the effort and graphic design of www.commonsense media.org, though parents who want to use their judgment-free ratings will have to get used to a more complex system of red, yellow, and green symbols and descriptions. The group offers an interesting manifesto, including the declarations, "We believe in media sanity, not censorship. We believe that media has truly become 'the other parent' in our kids' lives."

Movies Listed
by Age Group and Genre

★Tots

Animals
Finding Nemo (4+)
Little Bear Movie

Animation
Finding Nemo (4+)
The Little Bear Movie
My Neighbor Totoro (4+)
Toy Story

Classics
The Return of the Pink Panther

Comedy
The Return of the Pink Panther

★Kids

Action & Adventure
The Bear (6+)
Hidalgo
Jurassic Park (7+)
Superman

Animals
The Bear (6+)
Finding Nemo
Hidalgo
My Dog Skip

Animation
Finding Nemo
The Iron Giant (6+)
Kiki's Delivery Service (6+)
The Little Bear Movie

My Neighbor Totoro
The Sword in the Stone
Toy Story

Classics
The Return of the Pink Panther

Comedy
Big (7+)
Galaxy Quest (7+)
Meatballs (7+)
The Return of the Pink Panther

Drama
Fairy Tale: A True Story (6+)
Hoosiers (7+)
My Dog Skip
The Rookie
Searching for Bobby Fischer (7+)

Family Life
My Neighbor Totoro
Searching for Bobby Fischer (7+)
The Secret of Roan Inish (7+)
Time Bandits (7+)

Foreign
The Bear

Growing Pains
Meatballs (7+)

Sci-Fi & Fantasy
Fairy Tale: A True Story (6+)
Galaxy Quest (7+)
Jurassic Park (7+)
The Secret of Roan Inish (7+)
Time Bandits (7+)

Sports

Hoosiers (7+)
The Rookie

★Tweens (8–12)

Action & Adventure

The Bear
Butch Cassidy and the
Sundance Kid (10+)
Hidalgo
The Italian Job (10+)
Jurassic Park
Romancing the Stone (9+)
Superman
Touching the Void (10+)

Animals

The Bear
Finding Nemo
Hidalgo
My Dog Skip

Animation

Finding Nemo
The Iron Giant
Kiki's Delivery Service
My Neighbor Totoro
The Sword in the Stone
Toy Story

Classics

Butch Cassidy and the
Sundance Kid (10+)
The Return of the Pink Panther
Silent Running
Young Frankenstein (9+)

Comedy

Big
Butch Cassidy and the
Sundance Kid (10+)

Galaxy Quest
The Gods Must Be Crazy
Local Hero (12+)
Meatballs
The Return of the Pink Panther
Romancing the Stone (9+)
Starman (10+)
The Truman Show (9+)
Young Frankenstein (9+)

Documentary

Touching the Void (10+)

Drama

Breaking Away (10+)
The Champ
The Color of Paradise (9+)
Fairy Tale: A True Story
Hoosiers
I'm Not Scared (11+)
Kramer vs. Kramer
Little Man Tate
My Bodyguard
My Dog Skip
October Sky
The Outsiders (12+)
Phenomenon
The Rookie
Searching for Bobby Fischer
Sounder (10+)
Stand by Me (9+)
The Station Agent (12+)
What's Eating Gilbert Grape (10+)

Family Life

The Color of Paradise (9+)
Kramer vs. Kramer
Little Man Tate
My Bodyguard (9+)
My Neighbor Totoro
October Sky
Searching for Bobby Fischer
The Secret of Roan Inish

Sounder (10+)
Time Bandits
What's Eating Gilbert Grape (10+)

Foreign
The Bear
The Color of Paradise (9+)
I'm Not Scared (11+)
My Life as a Dog (9+)

Growing Pains
Breaking Away (10+)
Gregory's Girl (11+)
I'm Not Scared (11+)
Kramer vs. Kramer
Meatballs
My Bodyguard (9+)
My Life as a Dog (9+)
October Sky
The Outsiders (12+)
Stand by Me (9+)
What's Eating Gilbert Grape (10+)

Romance
Gregory's Girl (11+)
Romancing the Stone (9+)
Starman (10+)

Sci-Fi & Fantasy
The Andromeda Strain (11+)
Contact (9+)
Fairy Tale: A True Story
Galaxy Quest
Jurassic Park
The Secret of Roan Inish
Silent Running
Starman (10+)
Time Bandits

Sports
Breaking Away (10+)
The Champ
Heart of the Game

Hoosiers
The Rookie
Touching the Void (10+)

★Teens

Action & Adventure
The Bear
*Butch Cassidy and the
    Sundance Kid*
Hidalgo
The Italian Job
Jurassic Park
Romancing the Stone
Superman the Movie
Touching the Void

Animals
The Bear
Hidalgo
My Dog Skip

Animation
The Iron Giant
The Sword in the Stone
Toy Story

Classics
*Butch Cassidy and the
    Sundance Kid*
The Return of the Pink Panther
Silent Running
Young Frankenstein

Comedy
Big
*Butch Cassidy and the
    Sundance Kid*
Galaxy Quest
The Gods Must Be Crazy
Local Hero
Meatballs

The Return of the Pink Panther
Romancing the Stone
Starman
The Truman Show
Young Frankenstein

Documentary
Heart of the Game
Touching the Void

Drama
Breaking Away
The Champ
The Color of Paradise
Fairy Tale: A True Story
Hoosiers
I'm Not Scared
Kramer vs. Kramer
Little Man Tate
My Bodyguard
My Dog Skip
October Sky
The Outsiders
Phenomenon
The Rookie
Searching for Bobby Fischer
Sounder
Stand by Me
The Station Agent
What's Eating Gilbert Grape

Family Life
The Color of Paradise
Kramer vs. Kramer
Little Man Tate
My Bodyguard
October Sky
Searching for Bobby Fischer
The Secret of Roan Inish
Sounder
Time Bandits
What's Eating Gilbert Grape

Foreign
The Bear
The Color of Paradise
I'm Not Scared
My Life as a Dog

Growing Pains
Breaking Away
Gregory's Girl
I'm Not Scared
Kramer vs. Kramer
Meatballs
My Bodyguard
My Life as a Dog
October Sky
The Outsiders
Stand by Me
What's Eating Gilbert Grape

Romance
Gregory's Girl
Romancing the Stone
Starman

Sci-Fi & Fantasy
The Andromeda Strain
Contact
Fairy Tale: A True Story
Galaxy Quest
Jurassic Park
The Secret of Roan Inish
Silent Running
Starman
Time Bandits

Sports
Breaking Away
The Champ
Heart of the Game
Hoosiers
The Rookie
Touching the Void

The Andromeda Strain

★ GENRE: Sci-Fi & Fantasy

★ RATING: G

★ AGE: 11+

★ RUN TIME: 127 min.

★ AWARDS:
1972 Academy Award®: Best Art Direction nominee
1972 Academy Award®: Best Film Editing nominee
AFI®: Top 100 Thrills nominee

Watch how the scientists type a few characters into their computers and instantly come up with answers to life's most complicated technical questions. Remember, this was 1971—it took more than thirty years to arrive at a similar system with search engines such as Google.

Rated G, with disturbing images, brief nudity in a medical context, and mature themes; 1971; 127 minutes

A good choice for the budding scientist in the family

A movie doesn't need to be *Saw IV* or *Halloween 1001* to be unnervingly creepy.

If you want to give your older children that tingling gut-sense of disturbing science fiction without truckloads of blood and gore, rent *The Andromeda Strain* from way back in 1971.

A military space probe lands in remote New Mexico, apparently carrying a virus that wipes out an entire small town, save for a wailing baby and an old drunk. A top-secret, highly sophisticated investigative protocol swoops into place, sending the nation's top medical and scientific minds to a remote lab to study this horrific threat to all of humankind.

Best-selling author Michael Crichton is a Harvard Med School grad, and *The Andromeda Strain* is both a taut thriller and a careful reconstruction of the scientific method. Our heroes endure wicked decontamination before setting upon their analysis with plausible rigor.

As usual with Crichton's work, *Andromeda* is both enamored of science and skeptical of megalomaniacs who think they can harness nature for human "advancement."

While much of the movie is quietly methodical, there are some chilling moments, most notably when space-suited doctors explore the dead town. They cut open a victim's wrist, and crimson, powdered blood sifts out.

The Andromeda Strain is rated G, but it will be disturbing or simply dull for younger children. Save it for a tween or teenager with a willingness to try "old" movies.

The Bear

★ GENRE: Action & Adventure / Animals / Foreign

★ RATING: PG

★ AGE: 6+

★ RUN TIME: 93 min.

★ AWARDS:
1990 Academy Award®: Best Film Editing nominee

Male bears like the big grizzly in this film would naturally attack a young male cub and even eat it. To train their star for the filmmaking, director Jean-Jacques Annaud and his animal handlers gave Bart the Bear a stuffed bear cub to grow accustomed to before teaming him with costar Youk the Bear.

Rated PG for mild violence, injuries to animals; 1988; 93 minutes

A good choice for children 6 or older, and nature lovers of all ages

*B*elieve it or not, there are animal movies that don't involve cartoonish ocelots singing the praises of junk food or vicious anacondas terrorizing an entire town.

The Bear (1988) is a remarkable, almost dialogue-free nature film with a thrilling plot. Made by French director Jean-Jacques Annaud with highly trained animals and some modeling techniques, it tells the story of a little bear cub whose mother is crushed under a landslide while digging for honey.

The orphaned bear cub takes off cross country through stunning Canadian scenery and soon teams up with an enormous grizzly bear who is himself being chased by tenacious hunters. They strike up a partnership of sorts and lumber across the mountain slopes for more adventure. Annaud's film has nail-biting scenes of bears fording rivers, fighting cougars, and downing caribou, heeding the call of nature without turning it all into one big Disneyfied potty joke.

Humans, with their menacing guns and odd speech patterns, are mere interlopers in a landscape this large. Without being too heavy-handed about it, Annaud uses the hunters to explore questions of revenge versus live-and-let-live.

The movie is perfect for your animal-adoring children, but remember that the wild kingdom can be brutal: creatures get hurt in this film, and I have at least one young niece who would cringe at the sight of a bleeding dog.

3 *Big*

★ GENRE: Comedy

★ RATING: PG

★ AGE: 7+

★ RUN TIME: 104 min.

★ AWARDS:
   1989 Academy Award®: Best Actor nominee: Tom Hanks
   1989 Academy Award®: Best Writing Original Screenplay
      nominee
   AFI®: Top 100 Laughs
   AFI®: Top 100 Movies nominee

Just as Tom Hanks taps out a tune in the toy store, in an
episode of *The Simpsons*, Homer dances on a big, blow-up
piano keyboard.

Rated PG for mild language and mature themes; 1988; 104 minutes

A good choice for children 7 or older, and any parents who once desired to grow up faster

*B*ody-trading experiences make up a whole subgenre of movies, from Lindsay Lohan and Jamie Lee Curtis in the likable *Freaky Friday* remake to Steve Martin in the adult comedy *All of Me*. The list goes on: *Heaven Can Wait, Being John Malkovich, 13 Going on 30*, films that range from the very good to the utterly forgettable. But my favorite has always been *Big*, transformed by Tom Hanks from the pedestrian to the remarkably moving. Rather than apologize for his appealing boyishness, Hanks takes full advantage of it under Penny Marshall's direction to create a body-trapped role that appeals to adults and children in equal measure.

This 1988 film, which gave Hanks an Academy Award nomination, starts with childhood frustration. Visiting an amusement park, thirteen-year-old Josh asks an ominous fortune telling-machine called Zoltar to make him big. The next morning, Josh is a man, played by Hanks.

Big Josh has to flee his home and get a job in Manhattan, where he lands work at a cool toy company. His puppyish charm makes him successful with women for the first time, but this leads to complications. After living as a grownup for a time, he must decide whether to go home to his worried family or keep living the "big" life he thought he wanted.

As you watch Hanks, keep in mind the Hollywood rumor that Harrison Ford, Robert De Niro, and Robin Williams were all considered for the same part. It's hard to believe that any of them would have done half as well.

Breaking Away

★ GENRE: Drama / Growing Pains / Sports

★ RATING: PG

★ AGE: 10+

★ RUN TIME: 100 min.

★ AWARDS:

    1980 Academy Award®: Best Writing Original Screenplay

    1980 Academy Award®: Best Picture nominee

    1980 Academy Award®: Best Director nominee: Peter Yates

    1980 Academy Award®: Best Music Score nominee

    1980 Academy Award®: Best Supporting Actress nominee:
       Barbara Barrie

There really is a Little 500 bicycle race at Indiana University, patterned on the Indianapolis 500 auto race. *Breaking Away* is in the top 10 of the American Film Institute's 100 most inspiring movies.

Rated PG for some profanity; 1979; 100 minutes

A good choice for boys 10 and older, and for parents who appreciate Oscar-nominated work

Children destined at some point to feel trapped by their upbringing or their hometowns—everyone, in other words—should see *Breaking Away*.

This gem from 1979 never looks old, managing that elusive mix of sincerity, humor, plot, and character that lesser movies strive for. Down to the last frame—a freeze-shot of Paul Dooley reacting to yet more inspired foolishness from his son, Dennis Christopher—*Breaking Away* tells the story of a small town whose frustrations and joys are universal.

The four friends of *Breaking Away* have graduated from high school and immediately lost their way. They're from the working class of sleepy Bloomington, Indiana, ridiculed by the wealthier preppies at Indiana University, which dominates the town.

Christopher's character lives his fantasy of bicycle racing, even pretending to be Italian and adopting an Italian accent that impresses girls. A side bonus: the Italian shtick also drives his blue-collar father batty.

Christopher's charming lead role is well supported by a young and restless Dennis Quaid and character actors Daniel Stern and Jackie Earle Haley. All four bristle at their families' low expectations, yet they fear the possible failures entailed in "breaking away" from tradition.

A sleeper hit with the public, *Breaking Away* won a well-deserved Oscar for best screenplay.

Butch Cassidy and the Sundance Kid

✳ GENRE: Action & Adventure / Classics / Comedy / Westerns

✳ RATING: PG

✳ AGE: 10+

✳ RUN TIME: 110 min.

✳ AWARDS:
1970 Academy Award®: Best Music Song
1970 Academy Award®: Best Music Score
1970 Academy Award®: Best Cinematography
1970 Academy Award®: Best Writing Original Screenplay
AFI®: Top 100 Movies
AFI®: Top 100 Thrills

Robert LeRoy Parker was the birth name of the notorious robber who sometimes called himself Butch Cassidy. Henry Alonzo Longabaugh was the Sundance Kid. Most historians believe they died in a South American shootout after a series of daring robberies there, but some have speculated that "Butch" made it back to the United States and lived out his life in anonymity.

Rated PG for adult situations, profanity, and violence; 1969; 110 minutes

A good choice for children 10 or older, parents who want to relive the peerless Redford-Newman movie partnership

1t's not a movie-night special for the toddler set, or even for kindergarteners. (They don't give out medals for explaining even the tamest brothel scenes to preschoolers.) So save *Butch Cassidy and the Sundance Kid* for your older children, sit down with a big bowl of popcorn, and treat yourself to a Western full of action and charm.

Believe it or not, this 1969 classic is rated only PG, for some profanity, the brothel scene that is little more than a chaste conversation, and some old-fashioned shooting violence.

Director George Roy Hill accomplished his entertainment through great casting and dry wit, leavened by some well-placed slapstick routines. No need for gore or sex when you've got the chemistry of Paul Newman and Robert Redford and the pitch-perfect script of William Goldman.

Butch and Sundance blow up trains, high-tail it on horseback, quell rebellions in their own gang, and make nice with the pretty schoolteacher played by Katharine Ross. As another critic noted, a bonus is the bicycle-lesson scene to "Raindrops Keep Falling on My Head," which plays like a music video plunked down in the middle of a different movie.

My favorite scene has Sundance grinning at Butch after an explosion, paper money swirling around their heads: "Do ya think you used enough dynamite there, Butch?" Line deliveries like that, through an incandescent smile, turned Redford into a huge star.

The Champ

★ GENRE: Drama / Sports

★ RATING: PG

★ AGE: 8+

★ RUN TIME: 121 min.

★ AWARDS: 1980 Academy Award®: Best Music Score
  nominee

The Champ is a tale that has been retold many times, first by the great director King Vidor in 1931. That film was nominated for best picture and won Wallace Beery (in the role of an alcoholic prizefighter) the nod for best actor.

Rated PG for adult situations, emotional subject matter; 1979; 121 minutes

A good choice for children 8 or older, and parents who like a three-hankie weeper

My wife had been dying to show our kids one of her all-time favorite tearjerkers, the 1979 version of *The Champ*. At a house party, she finally got her chance: eleven girls, ages 11–14, lined up on our couch and looking for some entertainment.

Within an hour, ten of the girls were crying their eyes out, and the eleventh was blinking suspiciously fast. *The Champ* is a three-alarm, three-hanky movie of the highest order, perfect for your kids, who don't get to see many truly sad films.

Director Franco Zeffirelli makes beautiful pictures, from Shakespeare to a life of St. Francis. In *The Champ*, he imbues Florida with some old-time movie magic, retelling the tale of a washed-up former boxer trying to shed booze and gambling to win back his son.

Jon Voight plays Billy, a horse trainer who raises his son (Ricky Schroder, in his debut) around the pastel-colored racetracks of Florida. T.J.'s long-lost mother appears in the beatific form of Faye Dunaway, and she wants to raise him in the high society she has struggled to attain. To impress his son one last time, Billy fights an epic bout that threatens his life.

Spoiler alert, only to protect your most sensitive children: *The Champ* has one of the saddest endings in family movie history, and the middle has its shocking spots, too. But perhaps we protect our kids too much from sickness and danger. Seeing it onscreen in a safe family setting can bring out some important emotions.

The Color of Paradise

★ GENRE: Drama / Family Life / Foreign

★ RATING: PG

★ AGE: 9+

★ RUN TIME: 81 min.

Another terrific movie by director Majid Majidi, *Children of Heaven*, lost out to Roberto Benigni's *Life Is Beautiful* for the foreign language Oscar in 1998.

Rated PG for mature situations; 1999; 81 minutes

A good choice for children 9 or older with parents who can help on subtitles

The Color of Paradise might be the most visually stunning film your family will ever watch together.

My own clichéd images of Iran concern dusty streets and lingering footage of the hostage crisis. *The Color of Paradise* paints a rich portrait of the intensely green, flower-decorated countryside of Iran, teeming with bird songs and roaring streams. It also affords a view of family life in a distant society, one that goes beyond stereotypes of life in Muslim countries.

And it's a moving, simple story, just right for introducing your kids to subtitles. Young Mohammed is a blind student at a Tehran school, whose father from the country finds him a burden. Mohammed spends an idyllic summer in the hills with his sisters and grandmother, reveling in the green fields and deep woods. But his father would like to ditch Mohammed in order to remarry, and a potential tragedy looms.

Near the beginning of the film, Mohammed hears a fledgling bird fall from a tree and carefully restores it to the nest. Mohammed's joy at what he can do far outweighs the sorrow over his limitations. Director Majid Majidi captures blind Mohammed's sense of the world without condescension or melodrama.

Contact

★ GENRE: Sci-Fi & Fantasy

★ RATING: PG

★ AGE: 9+

★ RUN TIME: 153 min.

★ AWARDS:
   1998 Academy Award®: Best Sound nominee
   AFI®: Top 100 Thrills nominee

Contact is based on a novel by famed astronomer Carl Sagan, the lanky, nasal-voiced scientist from public television series such as *Cosmos*. He spent more than a decade helping to shape a film from his novel, then died seven months before *Contact* was finished. As the movie ends, the words "For Carl" appear before the credits.

Rated PG for adult situations, profanity, and violence; 1997; 153 minutes

A good choice for children 9 or older, and girls with a dream or in search of a dream

*T*he 1997 sci-fi thriller *Contact* moves in so many wonderful directions that it's hard to pick just one highlight.

It's an action-drama about the Earth's first possible contact with a species from another planet, with far richer characters than most blockbusters and a more optimistic outlook than, say, Stanley Kubrick's *2001*, another film older children will enjoy. *Contact* touches realistically on American science, politics, religion, and many other topics without appearing to be preachy or patronizing to any special interest.

But most important for parents of young girls, Jodie Foster's star turn as an ambitious yet humane astronomer is a role model for staying true to oneself.

Contact, based on a novel by the late populist astronomer Carl Sagan, is more than two and a half hours long and might take two nights of watching for many busy families. It's more than worth the effort, holding something for everyone: dazzling rocket sequences, sharply written public-policy arguments, and a testy, emotional relationship between Foster and Matthew McConaughey.

Foster's character believes she has discovered radio signals from intelligent life in outer space. She must fight overwhelming skepticism and petty careerists to win a fair hearing. Her quest becomes a worldwide cause, though director Robert Zemeckis (*Back to the Future*) never forgets to personalize each advance in science.

Fairy Tale: A True Story

★ GENRE: Drama / Sci-Fi & Fantasy

★ RATING: PG

★ AGE: 6+

★ RUN TIME: 99 min.

After he became the world's most famous magician, Harry Houdini spent much of his time debunking frauds and tricks by others. He argued that his tricks simply entertained people, while other charlatans were preying on fools with their destructive séances and other hoaxes.

Rated PG for mild, cartoonish violence; 1997; 99 minutes

A good choice for girls 6 or older, and for Anglophiles

*T*he British sensibility has a way of combining poignant childhood memories with troubling larger events, producing movies that bite far deeper than your average cartoon. *Fairy Tale: A True Story* (1997) is a great example, in the tradition of *The Little Princess, The Secret Garden*, or *The Chronicles of Narnia.*

Fairy Tale recounts the tale of young cousins Elsie and Frances in Britain, circa 1917, the time of the First World War. To escape their family demons—Elsie has lost a little brother, and Frances's father is missing on the front—they research fairy stories and act out elaborate fantasies in their garden.

They soon encounter what they believe to be real fairies and take a photograph that becomes the talk of all England. Are the creatures in the photo a miracle, or a hoax? Big names of the times weigh in on either side, with Peter O'Toole as Sir Arthur Conan Doyle and Harvey Keitel as Harry Houdini.

Without turning maudlin or preachy, *Fairy Tale* feels steeped in real emotions: fear, optimism, loss, hope. Perhaps the girls have made something up—but the adults around them seem to be making up stories all the time to insulate the girls and one another from the war. Whose truths or falsehoods hurt the most? Is there such a thing as too much fantasy? Or is reality overrated?

Finding Nemo

✕ GENRE: Animals / Animation

✕ RATING: G

✕ Age group: 4–9

✕ RUN TIME: 100 min.

✕ AWARDS:

2004 Academy Award®: Best Animated Feature

2004 Academy Award®: Best Music Score nominee

2004 Academy Award®: Best Writing Original Screenplay
nominee

2004 Academy Award®: Best Sound Effects Editing
nominee TIME® Magazine List: All-TIME 100 Movies

Finding Nemo won the best animated feature Oscar for 2003, an award category created in 2001 and first given to *Shrek*. Many fans argue more animated features should be considered seriously in the overall Best Picture category, though *Beauty and the Beast* was the only one to gain such a nomination, in 1991.

Rated G, for all audiences; 2003; 100 minutes

A good choice for children ages 4 to 9, and parents who appreciate animation style and a good, solid story

If *Toy Story* was the first warning from Pixar Studios that Disney would no longer overshadow the animation business, *Finding Nemo* (2003) was the final proof anyone needed. The international computer-generated blockbuster brought us undersea images so fresh, we forgot all about the Disney classic *The Little Mermaid.*

The look of *Nemo* is pure and the graphics unsurpassed by anything since, but again, the success of the movie rests on story, story, story. In this case, one of the oldest Hollywood stories: A road trip (or at least an East Australian Current trip) on the way to a rescue.

Nemo is a small clownfish whose neurotic father Marlin (Albert Brooks) has been trying to keep his little one safe ever since a predator snatched Mommy Nemo. But little Nemo is certain he's ready to swim with the bigger fishies, and ignores dad's warnings.

Nemo is captured by human divers and winds up in an aquarium in an Australian dentist's office. Marlin, meanwhile, has no one to help but the dim-witted blue surgeonfish Dory (voiced perfectly by Ellen DeGeneres), who is friendly but can't remember anything beyond five minutes ago. Thus Nemo becomes a sort of *Memento* for the younger set.

The two heroes set off in search of Nemo, variously assaulted or assisted by sharks, surfing turtles, and hungry seagulls. Kids of all ages love the brilliant shots of bright reefs and looming shipwrecks; teens and parents love the dude-speaking turtles and the harrowing trip through the jellyfish trap.

The success of *Finding Nemo* continued the Pixar erosion of partner Disney's domination of the animation business, and by the time Disney asked for a formal merger, Pixar headed the relationship. Pixar's people, including *Nemo* director Andrew Stanton, will likely fall under pressure to create a sequel to the hugely profitable original movie, but so far there are no plans to do so.

Galaxy Quest

★ GENRE: Comedy / Sci-Fi & Fantasy

★ RATING: PG

★ AGE: 7+

★ RUN TIME: 104 min.

In two scenes, you can see the actors mouth profanities, but the words are overdubbed with "full of it" and "screw that" to help *Galaxy Quest* keep a PG rating instead of moving up to the more restrictive PG-13.

Rated PG; 1999; 104 minutes

A good choice for children 7 and up, and parents who liked *Star Trek* or other sci-fi on TV

*G*alaxy *Quest* is a rousing adventure, a biting satire, and a warm lesson in friendship, all wrapped up in a science-fiction comedy that most people missed.

This treat from 1999 plays at one level to the kids, and at a richer level entirely to parents who lived through waves of *Star Trek*–style TV shows and spin-offs. That *Galaxy Quest* manages to be both cynical and sweet is a tribute to a writing and directing team little heard from since.

The film opens by introducing us to a bored and bickering team of washed-up actors, led by Tim Allen. He played Captain Peter Taggart on a now-defunct, cheesy sci-fi series called *Galaxy Quest*, and now he and his erstwhile crew spend their days signing autographs at geek conventions for people wearing Klingon costumes.

But real-life aliens have seen the TV show broadcast through space, and believe Taggart's heroics to be real. They need him to save their planet. It takes some doing to persuade Taggart, but once he's on board, Taggart brings along his fellow actors, portrayed hilariously by such talented players as Sigourney Weaver, Alan Rickman, and Tony Shalhoub.

"Never give up, never surrender!" is the battle cry. The friendly aliens have reproduced a working spaceship based on the fantasy physics of the TV show. Taggart and crew have to decide if they are brave enough to live up to their TV legends.

The parody of science fiction is note-perfect, sending up the genre while celebrating it at the same time.

The Gods Must Be Crazy

★ GENRE: Comedy

★ RATING: PG

★ AGE: 8+

★ RUN TIME: 109 min.

Look for later editions of the DVD that include documentary extras about the true way of life for modern Bushmen in southern Africa. Then your family can decide if *The Gods Must Be Crazy* is a shallow mistreatment of the indigenous, or simply a good-hearted romp.

Rated PG for brief nudity, adult situations, and language; 1981; 109 minutes

A good choice for children 8 or older, and anyone in search of a cultural experience or a debate about politically incorrect humor

N aïve, loopy, condescending, and inspired, *The Gods Must Be Crazy* is a goofy ride through the Botswana bush, offering something for everybody.

Parents will enjoy the 1984 hit's portrayal of an isolated Kalahari tribe boasting few material possessions. A glass Coke bottle falls from a passing airplane, and suddenly the tribe is split by envy, covetousness, and anger. They all want this useful piece of magic. How could such a simple object seem so important?

A bumbling romance develops, meanwhile, between a tongue-tied male biologist and a visiting teacher from the big city. A third plot offers a good dose of slapstick involving an attempted rebel coup, appealing to action-movie fans.

Finally, the family's skeptics can argue whether director Jamie Uys is celebrating the values of native culture, or coating them in paternal, potentially racist mawkishness.

The most intriguing plot of the movie, and the one that enchanted U.S. audiences when the foreign film arrived three years after it was made, follows tribesman Xi (played by a Uys-discovered tribesman named N!xau). Xi concludes the Coke bottle is an evil gift from the gods and must be thrown off the edge of the world. On his trek, he gets hopelessly mixed up in the madcap hijinks of the coup and the romance.

Watching *The Gods Must Be Crazy* these days can make you nostalgic for what seems like a distant era—the 1980s!—when a sweet, silly film swept the nation.

Gregory's Girl

★ **GENRE:** Growing Pains / Romance

★ **RATING:** PG

★ **AGE:** 11+

★ **RUN TIME:** 91 min.

★ **AWARDS:**
1982 BAFTA®: Best Film nominee
1982 BAFTA®: Best Direction nominee: Bill Forsyth

Gregory's Girl ranked Number 39 on *Entertainment Weekly*'s list of the top fifty high-school movies of all time. What was Number 1? *The Breakfast Club*, though many people would argue for *Rebel Without a Cause*, *Fast Times at Ridgemont High*, or *Election*.

Rated PG for brief topless nudity, some mild language; 1980; 91 minutes

A good choice for children 11 or older, and all parents

Adolescents love funny movies about adolescence, but their parents are usually looking for something with more redeeming qualities than *Porky's* or *American Pie.*

Which leads us to the more modest, yet far more realistic, pleasures of Bill Forsyth's *Gregory's Girl*, from 1980. Gregory (John Gordon Sinclair) is a gangly, acne-pitted specimen of teenage awkwardness at a typical Scotland high school, lending his dubious talents to a pathetic soccer team and wondering when a girl will actually talk to him.

In jogs star soccer player and feathered-hair hottie Dorothy (Dee Hepburn), who runs circles around the team and teases Gregory with the possibility of a date.

Forsyth, as I mention in touting *Local Hero* elsewhere in this book, tends to quietly inhabit the communities he features rather than elevate or critique them with his cameras. Gregory's optimism in the face of all evidence to the contrary is infectious, and it presents a reassuring view of the high-school years. Your kids will survive those transition years, and they'll even have a good time once in a while.

Gregory's Girl is rated PG, but to avoid surprises you should note that this was before Hollywood added PG-13. This movie is so innocent that it makes *American Pie* look like porn, but there is one early scene where Gregory and his friends catch a glimpse of a distant girl taking off her bra. The fact they have no idea what to do with this revelation is what makes Forsyth's film so appealingly true.

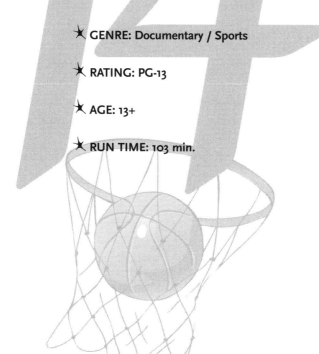

The Heart of the Game

★ GENRE: Documentary / Sports

★ RATING: PG-13

★ AGE: 13+

★ RUN TIME: 103 min.

Filmmaker Ward Serrill thought he was making a simple profile of a quirky high-school girls' basketball coach, but when Darnella Russell dribbled into the gym, Serrill ended up spending seven years with the team.

Rated PG-13, for mild profanity; 2005; 103 minutes

A good choice for any boy or girl remotely interested in sports, and anyone looking for motivation

amily-friendly movies with sports themes could take up a year's worth of columns, but for now I'm recommending my new favorite sports film, *The Heart of the Game.*

This unassuming, largely overlooked documentary from 2006 is the most riveting basketball tale you will find this side of *Hoosiers* and *Hoop Dreams*, and it has the advantage over those films of focusing on the girls' approach to the parquet floor. If someone had tried to write the ending of *The Heart of the Game* as fiction, directors would have laughed.

Because modernism made us suspicious of the possibilities of a happy ending, we spend much of this film dreading a depressing outcome. No need. You—and better yet your whole team of basketball- or soccer-playing girls who see it for motivation—will find plenty of uplift in *The Heart of the Game.*

The movie follows avuncular college professor Bill Resler as he builds a winning girls' basketball program in Seattle. The team first makes a run deep into the state playoffs, and then Darnella Russell dribbles into his gym.

Russell is black in a mostly white school. She is a problem child carrying a big chip and the doomed look of someone about to mess up. She's also the best player the state of Washington has seen, with Allen Iverson–style drives through the paint. Meanwhile, the girls thrive under Resler's silly motivational schemes, where he teaches them both to be good sports and to shout, "Sink your teeth in their neck! Draw blood!"

Resler promises that if they make it to the state championship game, every girl down to the lowliest benchwarmer will get to play. Meanwhile, Russell's problems explode into a meltdown and a court case. *The Heart of the Game* is an incomparable lesson in hard work, loyalty, team spirit, and forgiveness.

15

Hidalgo

★ GENRE: Action & Adventure / Animals

★ RATING: PG-13

★ AGE: 5+

★ RUN TIME: 135 min.

Star Viggo Mortensen likes to be the stoic cowboy-poet in real life, too, and he bought one of the American paint horses that were used to play *Hidalgo* in the movie.

Rated PG-13 for mild violence and sexual innuendo; 2004; 135 minutes

A good choice for children 5 or older, and horse lovers of all ages

Hidalgo is a modern version of the kind of rousing, completely illogical adventure movie that used to play downtown cinemas for generations of happy children. Right after the newsreel, a horse chase! And bad guys with rifles! And a tight-lipped, seen-it-all hero who'd rather save his horse than kiss a girl!

Too many families passed up this winner in 2004, but it's getting a well-deserved second life on cable and DVD.

The story follows American cowboy Frank Hopkins (Viggo Mortensen, of *The Lord of the Rings* fame) as he takes his mustang to a legendary race in the Arabian desert. Along the way, cruel rivals, gorgeous princesses, scheming rich ladies, and blinding dust storms beset Hopkins and Hidalgo. Mortensen has that cowboy way about him, and the drama is leavened by some old-fashioned sidekick humor.

Omar Sharif makes a welcome return to the movies as a sheikh whose daughter may have eyes for Hopkins. When your kids are older, give them the gift of the greatest desert movie of all time, *Lawrence of Arabia*, where Sharif stars alongside Peter O'Toole.

Some of the movie is even true: Hopkins was a renowned winner of long-distance horse races in the late 1800s.

Hoosiers

★ **GENRE:** Drama / Sports

★ **RATING:** PG

★ **AGE:** 7+

★ **RUN TIME:** 115 min.

★ **AWARDS:**

1987 Academy Award®: Best Music Score nominee
1987 Academy Award®: Best Supporting Actor nominee:
Dennis Hopper
AFI®: Top 100 Thrills nominee

Actor Maris Valainis, who plays team star Jimmy Chitwood, is the only actor making up the fictitious Hickory team who didn't play high school basketball.

Rated PG for mild violence, adult situations; 1986; 115 minutes

A good choice for children 7 or older, and all parents

*G*reat movie stories jump to a new level of mythology each time you're able to switch off the DVD player, turn to the kids, and say, "You know, that was all true."

At least most of it was true where the sports classic *Hoosiers* is concerned. *Hoosiers* changes the name of a tiny, basketball-crazed Indiana town from Milan to Hickory, but the most important details unreel as they actually happened in this winning heart-stopper from 1986.

A school with only seventy-three students truly did take its boys' basketball team all the way to the Indiana championship game in 1954, beating the largest city powerhouses at a time when the state threw all teams into one classification. Thanks to an understated, spot-on performance by Gene Hackman as a troubled coach, *Hoosiers* recreates those glory days with a minimum of schmaltz.

There are some nice filming touches you'd never notice: The movie's championship game is shot in the same big barn of a gym that hosted the real final game three decades before. Ray Crowe, who coached Indiana teams in the 1950s, plays the coach of the big-city school that Hickory goes up against in the final. The year after Milan won, Crowe led the first all-black team to the state championship.

17

I'm Not Scared

★ GENRE: Drama / Foreign / Growing Pains

★ RATING: R

★ AGE: 11+

★ RUN TIME: 110 min.

I'm Not Scared is loosely based on a real kidnapping of a child from Milan, an incident that was a major news story in Italy at the time.

Rated: R for disturbing images and subject matter; in Italian, with subtitles; 2003; 110 minutes

A good choice for children 11 or older, watching with their parents

Itchy adolescents love the film *Stand by Me*—discussed elsewhere in this book—because it helps them express an idea they carry around only half-formed: Maybe their parents are not perfect. Maybe they want to do some things differently from the way their parents do them.

A recent Italian movie shapes some of those same concepts into a gritty, surprising drama. *I'm Not Scared* features a boy who has to show courage without flinching from his new discovery that adults sometimes behave badly.

Young Michele lives in an isolated, sun-baked southern Italian village, bickering with his family and his friends. One night he makes a terrifying find: another young boy, chained in a pit and apparently held for ransom.

Who did it? What should Michele do to help? What if his own parents are involved? The film is all too literal, but it works on psychological levels, as well: Does the feral captive reflect some shadowy portion of Michele's personality yet to reveal itself?

I'm Not Scared is more disturbing than most family movies we recommend, but with your older tweens and teens, it is a thrilling drama. And it connects you with the Starz Denver Film Festival that takes over the city every November; *I'm Not Scared* was one of the top features in the 2003 version of the film fest.

The Iron Giant

★ **GENRE:** Animation

★ **RATING:** PG

★ **AGE:** 6+

★ **RUN TIME:** 86 min.

Director Brad Bird helped develop *The Simpsons* for TV before taking on *The Iron Giant*. He went on to win an animation Oscar for writing and directing *The Incredibles*.

Rated PG for mild, cartoonish violence; 1999; 86 minutes

A good choice for children 6 or older, and fans of old-school science fiction

*T*ired of the frenetic pace and hip-until-last-week pop-culture jokes of recent animated movies? Then dig in the archives all the way back to 1999, and enjoy Brad Bird's pre-*Incredibles* treasure *The Iron Giant*.

The young hero, Hogarth, is allowed to take long solo walks in the deep Maine Woods, searching for an alleged alien landing in paranoid 1957. His flashlight plays near and far, brighter and dimmer, across the landscape—and then it finds something. The story builds as Hogarth (voiced by Eli Marienthal) and the alien Giant (Vin Diesel) take their time getting to know each other.

Neither Hogarth nor we are won over by the winking musical numbers or cloying self-reference of recent animations like *Over the Hedge*. Instead, we're taken in by the giant's gentle manner, the nostalgic yet somehow realistic portrayal of a small Maine town, and the tactile pleasures of watching a metal titan snack on power poles and tin roofing.

For a long time, writer-director Bird (working from a Ted Hughes story and drawing on science-fiction classics such as *The Day the Earth Stood Still*) doesn't tell us why the giant crashed on the Maine shore. This mystery increases the tension as Hogarth races a klutzy federal agent (Christopher McDonald) to learn the giant's secrets.

What satire Bird employs is quiet. Hogarth loves B movies and scary comic books; his beatnik friend (Harry Connick Jr.) is a butt of jokes for being an artiste, but also a test of tolerance for locals. Don't miss Jennifer Aniston as the voice of Hogarth's mom—it may be some of her best work outside of *Friends*.

The Italian Job

★ **GENRE:** Action & Adventure

★ **RATING:** PG-13

★ **AGE:** 10+

★ **RUN TIME:** 111 min.

The Mini Coopers used for the amazing Los Angeles tunnel chases had to be retrofitted with electric engines, since the city doesn't allow gasoline combustion inside its subway tunnels.

Rated PG-13, for violence and some language; 2003; 111 minutes

A good choice for children 10 or older, fans of action thrillers

*M*ark Wahlberg is now a busy golden boy of the movies, starring in movies as diverse as Martin Scorsese's drama *The Departed*, the sports film *Invincible,* and the thriller *Shooter*.

Go back just a few years to find an adrenaline-rush of a Wahlberg movie for your older kids, a classic heist-and–double cross: *The Italian Job*, that 90-minute commercial for the Mini Cooper.

Your kids might recognize some of the heist-flick clichés: Wahlberg has the Brad Pitt or George Clooney part from *Ocean's Eleven*, and the sidekicks look similar, too. Mos Def has the Don Cheadle part, Jason Statham has the Scott Caan part. You could say Charlize Theron has the Julia Roberts part, but *The Italian Job* gives the Oscar-winning South African a little more burglary work to do.

The Italian Job is a remake of a 1969 Michael Caine movie with the same title, which is almost unwatchable now with all its mod-pants and slow pacing. There's a reason Austin Powers sent up that groovy era of filmmaking.

Director F. Gary Gray, who made a name for himself on music videos by OutKast and Ice Cube, has signed on with much of the crew for *The Brazilian Job*, scheduled for 2008.

Jurassic Park

★ **GENRE:** Action & Adventure / Sci Fi & Fantasy

★ **RATING:** PG-13

★ **AGE:** 7+

★ **RUN TIME:** 126 min.

★ **AWARDS:**
  1994 Academy Award®: Best Visual Effects
  1994 Academy Award®: Best Sound Effects Editing
  1994 Academy Award®: Best Sound
  AFI®: Top 100 Thrills

**Rated PG-13, for intense action sequences; 1993;
126 minutes**

**A good choice for kids 7 and up, who have older siblings or
cousins to cuddle with when the velociraptors show up**

Is it possible that *Jurassic Park* is already a decade and a half old? Every time I come across this taut thriller on cable TV, I stop to watch. The dinosaurs are as beautiful and terrifying as ever. The family of necessity, created by Sam Neill, Laura Dern, and the child actors Ariana Richards and Joseph Mazzello, gives the chills emotional heft.

Through the intelligent visages of Neill, Dern, Richard Attenborough, Samuel L. Jackson, and Jeff Goldblum, the fascinations of extreme science infuse the movie with a biting, optimistic level of curiosity.

Dern is one of director Steven Spielberg's most interesting heroines. Unlike other Spielberg women, Dern's scientist is a full character, smart and adventurous while never completely hiding a maternal streak that makes her so winning.

Attenborough invites dinosaur experts Neill and Dern to his jungle island, where he has cloned dinosaurs from petrified DNA. A storm and power outage set the monsters loose even as villain Wayne Knight is trying to sell the DNA formula to outsiders.

Jurassic Park has become a Thanksgiving TV staple, like *The Wizard of Oz*, for good reason. It's the perfect family-night video for seven-year-old brothers to hide behind their thirteen-year-old sisters for protection.

Jurassic Park held the all-time box office record for highest-grossing movie for a few years, until *Titanic* came along and soaked the competition.

Kiki's Delivery Service

★ **GENRE:** Animation

★ **RATING:** G

★ **AGE:** 6+

★ **RUN TIME:** 103 min.

Though director Hayao Miyazaki is a Japanese icon, this movie's urban scenes draw from cities around the world to make his ideal design. Influences on Kiki's town include Stockholm, Lisbon, San Francisco, Milan, and Paris.

Rated G, for all audiences; 1989; 103 minutes

A good choice for girls 6 to 10 and their Disney-weary parents

On a bleak winter's night, when your street ice has hardened into bulletproof ruts and you're stuffing area rugs into door cracks to stop the drafts, treat your family to the rich colors and flights of fancy in *Kiki's Delivery Service.*

No one captures the wonders of flying and the golden possibilities of adolescence quite like Japanese anime master Hayao Miyazaki. His *My Neighbor Totoro* is discussed elsewhere in this book. His *Spirited Away* not only won the 2002 Academy Award for animation, but also remains the highest-grossing film of any genre in Japan.

Kiki, voiced here by Kirsten Dunst on a DVD readily available from Netflix, Blockbuster, and other sources, is an adolescent witch in an unnamed modern nation where witches are a welcome part of everyday life. Rather than perform Harry Potter dark arts or Gandalfian wizardry, witches here provide minor miracles of convenience and service.

She's turned thirteen, and so it's time for Kiki to leave her loving family and find a town that needs her. She and her black cat (marvelous sarcasm voiced by the late Phil Hartman) soar on her broom to find adventure, puppy love, and a friendly bakery.

Miyazaki's 1989 masterpiece offers adventure without terror, personal growth without platitudes, and friendship without condescension. It's a wonderful story for girls, but don't count out boys, who will enjoy the numerous flight scenes and affectionate portrayals of cats and dogs.

My own happiness in researching the movie was in discovering how many Miyazaki movies I have yet to watch.

Kramer vs. Kramer

★ GENRE: Drama / Family Life / Growing Pains

★ RATING: PG

★ AGE: 8+

★ RUN TIME: 105 min.

★ AWARDS:

1980 Academy Award®: Best Picture

1980 Academy Award®: Best Director: Robert Benton

1980 Academy Award®: Best Actor: Dustin Hoffman

1980 Academy Award®: Best Writing Adapted Screenplay

1980 Academy Award®: Best Supporting Actress:
Meryl Streep

The indelible scene where Hoffman and his onscreen "son" Justin Henry fight over the right to eat ice cream was completely improvised by the two of them. Hoffman had recently been through his own divorce, and he helped shape the screenplay based on his experience.

Rated PG for brief nudity, language, mature subject matter; 1979; 105 minutes

A good choice for children 8 or older, and all parents

*K*ramer *vs. Kramer* is that rare combination: For the parents, an Oscar best-picture winner, and for your kids, a child's-eye-view story with no saccharine or soft-pedaling.

The arguments over divorce and relationships are intense and may be too much for sensitive younger children. But lessons about how parents can grow into new roles and how damaged lives can be repaired should be engrossing and reassuring to kids starting at about age 8. *Kramer vs. Kramer* is definitely a movie to watch together—your kids may well seek shelter under your arm, glad to know their own family enjoys more peace than the people on screen.

Dustin Hoffman, Meryl Streep, and Jane Alexander bring skill and warmth to important roles; Justin Henry clinched the deal as the young boy navigating his parents' bitter breakup. Streep, Alexander, and Henry were all nominated for supporting Oscars, and Streep won; Hoffman won best actor for the 1979 film, and Robert Benton won as director and screenwriter. Quite the awards shelf for one movie!

If nothing else, let your kids watch the infamous ice cream scene, where Henry and Hoffman face off over food tasting. To any child or parent who has ever argued at the dinner table, everything rings true.

Also keep an eye out for improvisation—Hoffman likes to keep his fellow actors on their toes. In the equally famous restaurant scene where Streep returns and infuriates her ex, she had no idea Hoffman was going to break a wine glass.

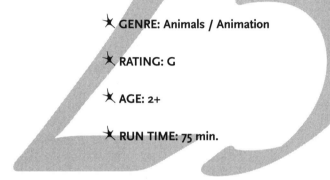

The Little Bear Movie

★ **GENRE:** Animals / Animation

★ **RATING:** G

★ **AGE:** 2+

★ **RUN TIME:** 75 min.

The Minarik / Sendak books on Little Bear have sold more than 6 million copies around the world. A TV series based on Little Bear and his friends runs periodically on the Nick Jr. cable channel.

Rated G, for all audiences; 2001; 75 minutes

A good choice for children age 2 to 5, and parents who want to sit with their kids for their first movie experience

Is there such a thing as a movie your three-year-old will watch that won't drive you completely bonkers? *Finding Nemo* comes to mind, and it's a terrific film, possibly the best animated movie of the past decade. But even that Pixar classic may have too many plot threads to hold your youngest child to her chair for that much-needed family breather.

From the time he was about twenty months old until he turned three, an undiscovered little gem called *The Little Bear Movie* made my son happy every time its lilting theme song reached his ears. It's based on the beloved stories by Else Holmelund Minarik, and illustrated by Maurice Sendak of *Where the Wild Things Are* fame. The movie animation is based on Sendak's drawings, and it follows the simple story of Little Bear's camping trip with his father and his discovery of a new friend in the wild.

The plot certainly won't stretch a parent's brain, and the bear family's interactions occasionally verge on cloying. But I enjoyed vegging out to this movie because of its loving depiction of that father-son camping trip, and because of terrific songs contributed by folk rocker Shawn Colvin. My wife and I have searched high and low for downloadable versions of her songs "It's a Great Big World" and "Everybody Wants to Paint My Picture." Don't laugh—you'll be addicted after one run-through.

After their camping trip, Little Bear invites a wild bear called Cub home to see how domestic life might suit him. Cub will eventually have to return to the wilderness, of course. Little Bear employs his cadre of creature friends, from Duck to Cat, to help with the transition.

Sometimes everybody in the family needs a short, quiet break from reality. *The Little Bear Movie* got us through some long snowy afternoons and some late nights with ear infections. That's more than enough to earn this parent's gratitude.

Little Man Tate

★ **GENRE:** Drama, Family Life

★ **RATING:** PG

★ **AGE:** 8+

★ **RUN TIME:** 99 min.

Jodie Foster was a whiz-kid herself, said to be a member of the high-IQ society Mensa. She was in TV commercials by age three and starred in a string of Disney movies beginning at age nine. Born in 1962, she's already had a forty-year show business career, including two Academy Awards.

Rated PG for mild language and mature subject matter; 1991; 99 minutes

A good choice for children 8 or older

*L*ittle Man Tate is about a genius kid trying to find his comfortable place in the world. But the kid who is most fun to watch in *Little Man Tate* is a cape-wearing math whiz with a potty mouth and a bad attitude.

Jodie Foster—yes, that Jodie Foster—combines these quirky elements into an entertaining tale of finding friends while staying true to yourself. *Little Man Tate* was Foster's second attempt at directing a movie, in 1991, and she costars as the blue-collar mother of a smartie played by Adam Hann-Byrd.

Fred Tate is a fourth-grader who can solve college-level math in his head and play complex piano concertos. But he has no one to hang out with. His immature but fiercely protective mom wants to help, but doesn't know how.

Fred is drawn to a genius school run by the uptight Dianne Wiest. That's where we meet the caped crusader, Damon, whose arithmetic IQ is as high as his emotional IQ is low. Damon ridicules Fred as the new runt on the smart block, but he also fears that Fred may supplant him as the school's wonder boy.

Foster tells a straightforward story in a restrained way, letting us get to know Fred without trying for Hollywood epiphanies. Surprisingly, she hasn't directed since, though she was set to helm a project called *Sugar Kings* in 2007.

25

Local Hero

★ GENRE: Comedy

★ RATING: PG

★ AGE: 12+

★ RUN TIME: 112 min.

★ AWARDS:
AFI®: Top 100 Movies nominee
1984 BAFTA®: Best Direction: Bill Forsyth
1984 BAFTA®: Best Film nominee
1984 BAFTA®: Best Supporting Actor nominee:
Burt Lancaster

Fans of *Local Hero* started showing up in the town where much of the movie was filmed, Pennan, on the Scottish coast. They wanted to see the bright red phone box where Mac makes so many calls, but the town didn't have one. So they imported one to make reality match up with the fiction.

Rated PG for adult situations; 1983; 112 minutes

A good choice for children 12 or older, and all parents who appreciate a quirky romance

Bill Forsyth movies could make up a whole chapter in any family movie book. When I first picked Forsyth's *Local Hero* as a family gem, the quiet, satisfying way it unfolds made me remember *Gregory's Girl*, *Comfort & Joy*, and *Housekeeping*.

We'll get to those other worthy films, eventually. For now, if you want a quirky, beautiful movie about people living happily at the edge of the world, start with *Local Hero*.

Peter Riegert, of *Animal House* fame, plays Macintyre, a real-estate buyer for a Texas oil company led by a loopy chairman, Felix Happer (a delightful Burt Lancaster). Happer smells oil in an isolated Scottish fishing village and sends Macintyre out to buy the whole town and beachfront.

Without resorting to slapstick, *Local Hero* is a fish-out-of-water tale that reverses course more than once. Far from feeling bamboozled, the savvy townspeople can't wait to take their millions. They are led by Urquhart (Denis Lawson), perhaps the smoothest and sexiest bed-and-breakfast owner in Scottish history.

Macintyre, meanwhile, falls in love with the scenery. Will commerce or companionship win out?

I've shown my kids movies like *Local Hero* and had to sit on them for the first half-hour—understated comedies seem slow to a generation trained on *Spider-Man* and *Grand Theft Auto*. But your older kids will appreciate this glimpse at another way of life, where people are cool and self-assured without being worldly.

Meatballs

★ GENRE: Comedy / Growing Pains

★ RATING: PG

★ AGE: 7+

★ RUN TIME: 92 min.

★ AWARDS: AFI®: Top 100 Laughs nominee

Bill Murray was one of the popular stars from the classic *Saturday Night Live* casts when he agreed to do *Meatballs*, in his first major film role. Legend has it Canada's Camp White Pine stayed open during the shoot, and the real campers and counselors were extras.

Rated PG for brief nudity, adult humor, and language; 1979; 92 minutes

A good choice for children 7 or older, goofballs of all ages

"Where's Tripper when you need him?" asks one Internet fan of the classic summer camp comedy *Meatballs.*

In the age of summer computer camps, all-star soccer training, and grammar cram courses, what all our kids need most is Bill Murray as a camp counselor, chanting, "It just doesn't matter! It just doesn't matter!"

With *Meatballs* (1979), director Ivan Reitman manages to find a tone at once sweet and realistic about loser kids and unambitious adults. The counselors at low-rent Camp Northstar are kind and concerned without seeming neutered; they'd just as soon skinny dip in the hot tub as give campers Rudy or Fink a pep talk.

The action is a perfect underdog story. Northstar's underachievers have to compete in end-of-summer games with snobby Camp Mohawk. Tripper starts jogging with depressed Rudy to shake him out of his funk, and of course the contests must conclude with Rudy taking on Camp Mohawk's smug running champ in a cross-country duel.

The rapport between Murray and Chris Makepeace as Rudy is genuine and moving, with Murray never letting it go sappy. Legend has it that counseling centers have used *Meatballs* as instructional video on how to reach unhappy kids.

Makepeace has an intelligent, puppy-dog face highly suited for movies like this one, as well as the excellent *My Bodyguard,* which we'll highlight in another entry.

Meatballs will make you think twice about eating another hot dog, but there's no better family preparation for a season of dubious campouts.

My Bodyguard

★ GENRE: Drama / Family Life / Growing Pains

★ RATING: PG

★ AGE: 9+

★ RUN TIME: 96 min.

Director Tony Bill found a seamless tone for his work in
My Bodyguard, but his career hasn't had big highlights since.
His movie *Flyboys*, about World War I fighter pilots, was one
of the dumbest films of 2006.

Rated PG, with some mild language; 1980; 96 minutes

A good choice for children 9 to 13, and for parents interested in one of the better high-school movies of all time

*T*his quietly entertaining showdown movie gives us good guys confronting bad guys, high-school misery, budding friendship, eccentric parenting, and one of the most satisfying, triumphant endings ever crafted for an adolescent film.

Chris Makepeace, previously of *Meatballs* fame, is a small guy named Clifford in a big new high school in Chicago. His dad, played by Martin Mull, is the distracted manager of a big hotel; Clifford enjoys hotel living with his silly grandmother, played by the inimitable Ruth Gordon.

School is a trial for young Clifford. The hallways are controlled by a bully named Moody, expertly represented here by Matt Dillon. Moody and his gang demand money to "protect" the kids from an allegedly worse bully, the hulking, silent Linderman (Adam Baldwin). But Clifford decides to take a different tack: he approaches the elusive Linderman and tries to hire him as his bodyguard against Moody. Linderman agrees for a while, but he is haunted by his own troubled past, which includes a little brother who died in mysterious, much-rumored circumstances.

The absence of adults who will do anything about Moody and the slumping unhappiness of high-school kids who can't wait for their purgatory to end give *My Bodyguard* a realistic edge. Friendships wax and wane, bullies come and go, and there is no magical solution to a problem. Sooner or later, Clifford will have to stand up for himself against Moody, and we're never quite sure how that will turn out.

Watch *My Bodyguard* with your adolescents and ask them if the high school scenes ring true; if so, you may want to make a school visit. If not, you can breathe a sigh of relief that bullies are no longer indulged at most big high schools.

My Dog Skip

★ GENRE: Animals / Drama

★ RATING: PG

★ AGE: 5+

★ RUN TIME: 95 min.

Memoirist and novelist Willie Morris wrote poetically of his childhood in Yazoo, Mississippi, in a number of acclaimed works, including *North Toward Home*. He saw an advance screening of *My Dog Skip*, based on his work, and enjoyed it, but he died of a heart attack just before the movie opened to great success across the nation.

Rated PG for some mild language and mature subject matter; 2000; 95 minutes

A good choice for children 5 or older; anyone who ever loved a pet

*G*rown men cry like babies at the ending of *My Dog Skip*, proving that the love of a childhood pet makes for both great memories and great movies.

This boyhood movie from 2000 touches many of the familiar bases of eccentric Southern growing-up stories: eggheads, bullies, baseball, moonshiners, war veterans, dreamy girlfriends, and cute puppies. Yet it adds just enough unexpected material to elevate *My Dog Skip* into a classic as was the memoir it is based on, by Pulitzer Prize–winning writer Willie Morris.

Frankie Muniz, best known for his work in the television series *Malcolm in the Middle*, plays young Willie as a scrawny, bookish kid picked on by popular classmates. Mom (Diane Lane) finally convinces stoic dad (Kevin Bacon) that a pet would help, and introducing Skip into Willie's life changes everything for the better.

Adding depth to the story is next-door neighbor Dink Jenkins (Luke Wilson), a star athlete who goes off to fight in World War II. Willie idolizes him, but Dink comes back labeled as a coward. Dink explains to Willie, "It ain't the dyin' that's scary. It's the killin'." Willie's dad was a war hero in the Spanish Civil War, and he tries to tell Dink why Willie still looks up to him.

"You're his hero because you're his friend," the dad says, and that's wise advice for all of us listening.

Besides the talented human cast, you and your kids may recognize Skip as well. The older version of the dog is played by Moose and his son Enzo, Jack Russell terriers who also starred in the sitcom *Frasier*.

My Life as a Dog

★ GENRE: Foreign / Growing Pains

★ RATING: NR

★ AGE: 9+

★ RUN TIME: 101 min.

★ AWARDS:
1987 Golden Globe: Best Foreign-Language Film
1987 Independent Spirit Award: Best Foreign Film
1987 New York Film Critics Circle: Best Foreign Film

The true story of Laika the space dog will make for an interesting ethics conversation with your kids. The first living creature successfully launched into space, Laika nevertheless died a few hours after reaching orbit. Some scientists and many animal rights activists were angry about the treatment of Laika, a stray plucked from Moscow's streets.

Not rated, though deserving a PG or mild PG-13 for some sexual content; 1985; 101 minutes

A good choice for children 9 or older willing to read subtitles, and for all parents in search of a genuinely moving story

Nobody seems to want young Ingemar hanging around, but the angel-faced, mournful little Swedish boy has a life-affirming philosophy: Things could always be worse. For example, he muses aloud, as he hides under furniture to avoid his mother's rantings, you could be that guy who took a walk in a field near a track meet and got impaled by a javelin. Or, even more heartbreaking, you could be Laika, the Soviet dog sent into space in a Cold War experiment. The experiment worked, the Soviet scientists were heroes, and yet the poor dog died alone above the atmosphere.

It's a series of emotionally wrenching moments like these that made *My Life as a Dog* such a transatlantic hit when it arrived in foreign-film art houses in 1985. It cemented the American idea of quirky but lovable Scandinavians, and launched writer-director Lasse Hallström's brilliant career as a creator of warm, emotionally rich films. (Hallström went on to helm *What's Eating Gilbert Grape*, discussed elsewhere in this book, as well as *The Ciderhouse Rules, Chocolat*, and many more fine movies.)

Ingemar is 12, and his ailing mother needs a break. She ships him off to a rural town, where the boy enjoys his uncle's company and starts a mutual crush with a tomboy named Saga, who can't decide whether to kiss Ingemar or punch him in the nose. She does both.

As with so many movies about adolescent boys, dogs play a big part. Not only does Ingemar muse about the fate of Laika; he also worries about his own beloved dog, lost in the shuffle as Ingemar shuttles between relatives. When things get too much for him, Ingemar starts acting like a dog himself, clinging to ankles and barking madly.

Like *The Color of Paradise*, *My Life as a Dog* is a good starter movie for family members willing to try subtitled foreign films for the first time. You can easily follow the action and the sentiment, without catching every single word.

My Neighbor Totoro

★ GENRE: Animation / Family Life

★ RATING: G

★ AGE: 5+

★ RUN TIME: 87 min.

Ken Jennings, the most successful contestant ever on the TV game show *Jeopardy*, is said to have carried a small plush toy of Totoro around in his back pocket for good luck.

Rated G; 1988; 87 minutes

A good choice for children 4 to 9, anyone looking for a new style of animation

My Neighbor Totoro is a dreamy, soul-hugging adventure for children, and a soothing respite for parents after a long day of too much thinking.

This 1988 animated beauty from Hayao Miyazaki bears little resemblance to the recent frenetic animations of Disney or Pixar, all stuffed with self-satisfied pop-culture detritus. Miyazaki is more interested in the solemn allure of a long flight of stairs up to the attic, or dragonflies skimming across a woody creek. His renderings of a forest-edge bus stop in the rain will make you long for an umbrella and a pair of boots to stomp in puddles.

In Japanese legend, a Totoro (pronounced TOE-ta-row) is a lazy, furry woodlands troll. In this story, two sisters move with their father to a decrepit country house, waiting for their mother to join them from a long illness in hospital.

Miyazaki and the girls explore the gorgeous Japanese countryside in minute detail, as they avoid their worries with long Rambles through the branches. When they stumble across the noisy Totoro and his friends, they are enchanted instead of terrified.

Those of us traumatized by too many Asian horror movies lately can appreciate Miyazaki's tranquil depiction of rural life in Japan. There are no psychotic ghosts in this gentle film. The girls' idyll, made bittersweet by their ailing mother, is a tonic for our times.

The Disney dub of the movie wisely employs the voices of Dakota Fanning and her sister Elle, to avoid subtitles and replace an earlier voiceover.

31

October Sky

★ GENRE: Drama / Family Life / Growing Pains

★ RATING: PG

★ AGE: 8+

★ RUN TIME: 108 min.

Homer Hickam Jr.'s book *Rocket Boys* was a critical and commercial success. In addition to his career as a top NASA scientist, he has written popular accounts of the U-boat battles in World War II and of his lifelong love of scuba diving.

Rated PG for mild language, adult situations; 1999; 108 minutes

A good choice for children 8 or older, and for parents hungry for an uplifting story

Restraining the sentimental from taking that fatal last step into the maudlin is one of the toughest tricks in the movie business. The small-town triumph movie *October Sky* succeeds by carefully holding to its own boundaries of gritty nostalgia.

Jake Gyllenhaal makes his lead debut in this 1999 drama, based on the memoir of NASA engineer Homer Hickam Jr. High-school boys in a 1950s West Virginia coal mining town are mesmerized by the Russian launch of the Sputnik satellite and decide to teach themselves the principles of rocketry.

Young Homer's dreams are checked by his seething, overworked father (Chris Cooper), who spends his days in backbreaking labor underground or fighting management battles over safety and wages. Laura Dern counters Cooper's fury with encouragement, as a teacher betting her boys can learn a future more promising than mining.

Director Joe Johnston's assured sense of pacing lets us see the town of Coalwood as both a nest for Homer and a trap. As in equally praiseworthy movies such as *Breaking Away*, Homer must fight his family and his community before he can begin to understand how much he needs them.

If you can hold back your emotions during the moving father-son ending of *October Sky*, you might need to get your pulse checked. The conclusion seems just right and should give the movie enough depth for everyone to enjoy.

The Outsiders

★ GENRE: Drama / Growing Pains

★ RATING: PG-13

★ AGE: 12+

★ RUN TIME: 91 min.

The Outsiders is a favorite novel of middle-school and high-school kids. One class was asked who should direct the movie. It voted for Coppola and sent him a letter along with S. E. Hinton's novel. That's what got him started on the project.

Rated PG-13 for fighting violence, some language, mature subject matter; 1983; 91 minutes

A good choice for boys 12 or older, and for Francis Ford Coppola fans

Francis Ford Coppola's *The Outsiders* is far grittier fare than we usually recommend for movie night. But if you choose your family audience carefully, the dark 1983 adaptation of S. E. Hinton's popular adolescent novel can be a remarkable movie experience.

Like another Coppola-Hinton collaboration from that year, *Rumble Fish, The Outsiders* reveals another world, far from our relatively safe cities: angry, blue-collar teens growing up on the poor side of the tracks as "Greasers" in an Oklahoma city in the 1960s. (The movie was filmed in Tulsa.) Their lives are defined by their emotional and physical battles with the city's rich kids, nicknamed "Socs." Few directors besides Coppola would have the guts to sustain the hopeless, class-warfare tone of Hinton's original novel.

Show your teens the work of a visionary, perfectionist director; meanwhile, they'll enjoy early-career looks at an amazing roster of future stars, including Matt Dillon, Rob Lowe, Emilio Estevez, Patrick Swayze, Ralph Macchio, Tom Cruise, and Diane Lane.

Fair warning: the fight scenes are brutal. Their redeeming value is that they add up to an honest antiviolence message, in contrast to Hollywood movies that pretend to critique violence while glorifying it with beautiful pictures.

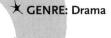

Phenomenon

★ **GENRE:** Drama

★ **RATING:** PG

★ **AGE:** 8+

★ **RUN TIME:** 124 min.

John Travolta was no precocious scholar in real life. He dropped out of high school to head for New York and a start on Broadway. To show your kids another side of the megastar in his younger days, sing along with *Grease* as another great family film.

**Rated: PG for some profanity and mature subject matter;
1996; 124 minutes**

A good choice for children 8 or older

1 didn't mean to do it, but now I notice a theme developing here: I must have a thing for movies about unexpected genius.

Mostly because I'd like to have it. Oh well. In the tradition of recommending *Little Man Tate* and *Searching for Bobby Fischer* elsewhere in this guide, we now reach for one of John Travolta's sweetest and most appealing roles, in *Phenomenon* from 1996.

Travolta is a small-town California car mechanic named George, living the good life among an enjoyable cast of character-friends played by the likes of Robert Duvall, Forest Whitaker, and Kyra Sedgwick. One night, George appears to be struck down by a blinding light. He starts reading a few books a day, learns whole languages in minutes, and he may have some ideas for the universities about nuclear fusion.

Where did George's new gift come from? Is it truly a gift, or a curse, if his friends can't handle the new George? Will the FBI consider the talkative genius some kind of threat?

Phenomenon boasts an easy friendship among the talented cast and a quiet sense of melancholy that precludes a flashy Hollywood ending. It's an adult story that your kids can appreciate.

And we'll let you know when there are enough "genius" movies to make a boxed set. Let's see: there's *Weird Science*, and *Real Genius*, and . . .

The Return
of the Pink Panther

★ GENRE: Comedy / Classics

★ RATING: G

★ AGE: Any

★ RUN TIME: 115 min.

In the earlier Pink Panther movies, Peter Sellers didn't goof around nearly as much with his French accent or the mispronounced words.

Rated G, with some risqué humor and slapstick violence; 1975; 115 minutes

A good choice for everybody in the family, grandma and grandpa, too, and anybody with a shred of a sense of humor

We recently crowded into a popcorn-infused living room at a lake house for a special edition of movie night, during a family reunion. On hand were cousins ranging in age from two to fifteen, and parents and grandparents from their forties into their seventies. The feature we chose was *The Return of the Pink Panther*.

We soon found out that the humor of Peter Sellers knows no age boundaries. His 1975 turn as bumbling detective Clouseau was his best in the *Pink Panther* run. *Return* has all the silliness a child needs and all the sly Euro-wit that an adult might want. If you can't laugh when Peter Sellers asks whether you have a license for that "moon-key," then comedy is just not the genre for you.

Directed by Blake Edwards as the third Panther movie following *The Pink Panther* and *A Shot in the Dark*, this one features some of the most memorable slapstick scenes in modern film humor. For that "chimpanzee monkey" scene, Clouseau interrogates a blind organ grinder about the legality of his pet, completely oblivious to the bank robbers plying their evil trade just over his left shoulder. Elsewhere, Clouseau, disguised as a hotel maid, sucks a pet bird into a vacuum cleaner and loses his pants while allegedly making a phone repair. These scenes are classic highbrow slapstick, and consistently appear on cranky critics' lists of favorite comedy routines.

But *Return* also hooks tweens with a tour-de-force opening scene, when the masked burglar goes through elaborate shenanigans to lift a storied diamond from a museum. The sequence was honored and parodied beautifully in the Wallace & Gromit animated short *The Wrong Trousers*.

Romancing the Stone

★ GENRE: Action & Adventure / Comedy / Romance

★ RATING: PG

★ AGE: 9+

★ RUN TIME: 110 min.

★ AWARDS:
1985 Academy Award®: Best Film Editing nominee
AFI®: Top 100 Thrills nominee
AFI®: Top 100 Laughs nominee

Director Robert Zemeckis has an incredible string of hits to his credit, such respectable popcorn flicks as *Back to the Future*, *Contact*, *Forrest Gump*, and *Castaway.* He teamed with Kathleen Turner on another hit, when she supplied the sex-kitten voice of Jessica Rabbit in *Who Framed Roger Rabbit?*

Rated PG for mild violence and profanity, brief nudity, adult situations; 1984; 110 minutes

A good choice for children 9 or older, and anyone in search of an old-fashioned matinee romp-and-romance

*T*he Robert Zemeckis classic *Back to the Future* gets a ton of play on family movie nights and cable rotation, but his romantic action comedy *Romancing the Stone* deserves a lot more airtime, and showcases marquee acting from some of the biggest names of the 1980s.

Kathleen Turner plays a mousy, city-based author of bodice-ripper novels, writing what she doesn't know: romance and adventure. Suddenly, a South American treasure map falls into her hands, and she must travel to rescue her antiquities-hunting sister.

In storied Cartagena, Colombia, she links up with mercenary hunk Michael Douglas in search of a priceless jewel. Bad guy Danny DeVito spices up the cynicism and danger.

The onscreen chemistry and snappy writing made a blazing star out of Turner and boosted Douglas's career; they reminded admirers of historic duos like Bogie and Bacall, or William Powell and Myrna Loy. Their sexy bickering in the jungle also conjures images of Bogie and Katharine Hepburn in *The African Queen*.

Looking back, 1984 was a terrific year for fun family movies, from *Ghostbusters* and *Gremlins* down the box-office list through *Karate Kid*, *Indiana Jones and the Temple of Doom*, *Footloose*, and *Splash*. Sounds like the lineup for a PG film festival all its own.

The Rookie

36

★ GENRE: Drama / Sports

★ RATING: G

★ AGE: 5+

★ RUN TIME: 127 min.

A minor league look-alike was used in *The Rookie* when the script called for a fastball, but Dennis Quaid did most of his own throwing. The filmmakers used a trick called "whip pans" to make his pitches look even faster. The real Jim Morris has a cameo as an umpire.

Rated G; 2002; 127 minutes

A good choice for children 5 or older, and sports fans of all ages

If Major League Baseball is the sport of choice for mom or dad, but the kids won't sit still for a four-hour Rockies game, there's more than one way to bring the whole family into your obsession.

A thoroughly winning performance by Dennis Quaid lifted *The Rookie* far above its sports-movie peers in 2002. Like Kevin Costner, Quaid has the build and the walk of a real athlete, and even more than Costner, Quaid knows how the timing of a warm smile can reassure his whole family.

Quaid inhabits the real-life tale of Jim Morris, a high-school science teacher in a rural Texas district who coaches the baseball team. He tells his underachieving boys that if they start living up to their potential, he'll try out again for the major leagues, twelve years after an injury ended his career.

It wouldn't be much of a story if Morris had failed, but of course he doesn't. The charm of *The Rookie* is how screenwriter Mike Rich forces Quaid to keep his family involved the entire way. Not only does Morris have to confront his father's scorn, but he also hasn't leveled with his wife (Rachel Griffiths) about the tryouts, and so he has to change a wailing baby's diapers when it's his turn to pitch.

For those of us over forty, there are plenty of "old man" insults that hit close to home.

Rich also wrote a satisfying screenplay for *Miracle*, another good family movie about the improbable 1980 U.S. Olympic hockey victory in 1980.

Searching for Bobby Fischer

★ GENRE: Drama / Family Life

★ RATING: PG

★ AGE: 7+

★ RUN TIME: 110 min.

★ AWARDS:
 1994 Academy Award®: Best Cinematography nominee

Josh Waitzkin and his real-life family members have cameos throughout the movie. The real-life chess teacher that Ben Kingsley's character is based on is said to be much kinder and humane than the fictional version invented here.

Rated PG, but some issues may go over the youngest children's heads; 1993; 110 minutes

A good choice for children 7 and older; all parents, especially competitive ones

In a world where competitive sports camps recruit six-year-olds, *Searching for Bobby Fischer* is the perfect movie to make a family think about the tradeoffs of winning, losing, and staying human.

This PG-rated jewel is a fictionalization of the real-life chess wizardry of six-year-old Josh Waitzkin. A well-adjusted New York boy with a love of baseball, Waitzkin (Max Pomeranc) sees street hustlers playing speed chess in Central Park and gets hooked on the game. His father, played with understated intensity by Joe Mantegna, senses a prodigy.

The movie's best scene has Mantegna testing Josh's potential skills. Dad sits alone at a chessboard in the living room. Josh is in the bathtub, playing with action figures, and calling out chess moves because he doesn't need to see the board to win. Mom (Joan Allen) listens and rolls her eyes in the kitchen. The timing of writer-director Steven Zaillian's payoff is perfect.

Josh likes to win, but he also likes being a decent person. His parents want him to live up to his potential, but they cringe at the rabid chess-parents they meet. Laurence Fishburne and Ben Kingsley play spot-on supporting roles as two very different kinds of chess teachers.

Zaillian, who won the Oscar for writing *Schindler's List* the same year (1993), creates tension without going Hollywood. As Josh ponders what kind of chess player—and more important, what kind of boy—he wants to be, he also tells the story of mercurial American champ Bobby Fischer, adding a sense of melancholy to each victory.

Searching for Bobby Fischer is a movie with more than enough meat, potatoes, and emotion to satisfy everyone in the family.

The Secret of Roan Inish

⭐ **GENRE:** Family Life / Sci-Fi & Fantasy

⭐ **RATING:** PG

⭐ **AGE:** 7+

⭐ **RUN TIME:** 103 min.

⭐ **AWARDS:**
   1996 Independent Spirit Awards®: Best Director nominee:
   John Sayles
   1996 Independent Spirit Awards®: Best Feature nominee

People who love *Roan Inish* are surprised to learn the remaining filmography of director John Sayles, who rarely makes family-friendly movies. Sayles is better known for intense dramas like *Eight Men Out*, *Matewan*, and *Lone Star*.

Rated PG for some scenes that will need explaining to small children; 1994; 103 minutes

A good choice for children ages 7 and up who can sit still for a movie that unfolds at its own pace

Movie fans often ask me to endorse one of their favorites, the John Sayles–Haskell Wexler collaboration *The Secret of Roan Inish* (1994), as a poetic family film.

If you choose it for movie night, tell the kids to relax and wait for a plot to unfold. *Roan Inish* does not give up its secrets quickly, but the cinematography of Wexler on the Irish islands off the Donegal coast will entrance viewers of all ages who are willing to give it a chance.

The plot follows ten-year-old Fiona as she joins her grandparents in a tiny fishing village after World War II. She learns that storytelling and mythmaking are a way of life in a remote place, where the changing weather serves as their version of television and hardship is the master of everyone.

Fiona had a little brother who washed out to sea in a cradle, and the legend of the Selkies—part human, part seal—comes to dominate her time on the island. Sayles trusts his deliberate pacing to great effect, and he allows Wexler to become a star of the movie by the way he points his cameras. (Wexler was one of Hollywood's greatest cinematographers, having brought us *Bound for Glory, Days of Heaven*, and *One Flew Over the Cuckoo's Nest*, among others.) We discover magic right alongside Fiona.

If you've been trying to steer the family toward a trip to Ireland, this is the movie to put in the video slot.

Silent Running

★ GENRE: Classics / Sci-Fi & Fantasy

★ RATING: G

★ AGE: 8+

★ RUN TIME: 90 min.

Double-leg amputees played the lovable robot drones. They walked on their hands, an unusual motion that gives the robots a fascinating cross between human and otherworldly characteristics.

Rated G originally, but with mild profanity, limited violence, and issues of suicide; 1971; 90 minutes

A good choice for tweens and teens interested in the environment or space

*J*ust a few years ago, the science fiction cult classic *Silent Running* seemed hopelessly dated and melancholy, in a depressed-hippie, drank-the-bongwater kind of way.

Now that even the most diehard resistors have accepted the fact of global warming and even the oil companies are proposing solutions, the idea of Earthlings shipping their last surviving forests off into space on freighter ships seems prescient and intriguing.

If you have teenagers who are starting to read up on global warming and wondering what kind of planet their parents and grandparents have left them, *Silent Running* will make poignant and thought-provoking family viewing. Your littler ones may enjoy the robot-drones created by director Douglas Trumbull, who found double-leg amputee actors who could walk on their hands. Their motion is at once startling and unmistakably human.

In this dystopian future circa 1972, Earth has lost all its plant life, and the last gardens have been placed for safekeeping on freighter-domes. Bruce Dern plays an astronaut-botanist taking care of his beloved plants inside a dome orbiting Saturn. Radio orders tell Dern and his colleagues that their mission has been scuttled.

Though his fellow astro-cowboys are dying to get back to Earth, Dern wants to preserve the forests. He must contemplate the morality of human life versus plant life.

Trumbull previously helped Stanley Kubrick create the timeless special effects for *2001: A Space Odyssey*. Trumbull perfected the look of Saturn, rejected by Kubrick in favor of Jupiter, and filmed his interiors on the mothballed aircraft carrier. A terrific set of extras on the DVD, available through Netflix or Blockbuster, gives great insight into how the production went together.

Sounder

★ GENRE: Drama / Family Life

★ RATING: NR

★ AGE: 10+

★ RUN TIME: 105 min.

The novel *Sounder*, by William H. Armstrong, won the Newberry medal for best children's fiction in 1970. The book actually has a far more depressing ending than the movie version.

Unrated, but PG for mature subject matter; 1972; 105 minutes

A good choice for children 10 or older, and all families looking to see how the other half used to live

*T*hink about what our children see in today's family movies: Lives of relative abundance, people with nearly universal access to homes, cars, full cupboards, electronic devices spilling out the doors.

You don't have to wait for a visit to the pioneer museum to show them a time and place where life was a daily struggle to put food on the table. *Sounder* takes us straight to the sharecropping fields of rural Louisiana during the Depression, when success for many black families was finding a piece of meat to add to the stewpot.

The award-winning children's book and the 1972 film were named after a dog, but Sounder plays a bit part in this methodically paced family drama. Eldest son David loves to hunt raccoons with his father (the magnificent Paul Winfield) and enjoys the freedom of rural life, even as his family fights brutal poverty. Pop soon steals a ham, and the sheriff drags him off to the work farm.

It may be hard for your children to imagine, but making the mental leap will open their minds. This family has no money, no car, no education, no power to demand answers. If David wants to visit his father in prison, he must trek for days across the countryside, looking at a map he can't read.

David stumbles across a school for black children, something he's never seen, and suddenly his life has the chance to move in new directions. Meanwhile, director Martin Ritt soaks us in the heat, the beauty, the racism, and the buzzing cicadas of steamy Louisiana.

Sounder was nominated for best picture and a host of other awards, including best adapted screenplay, best actor for Winfield, and best actress for mom Cicely Tyson.

Stand By Me

★ GENRE: Drama / Growing Pains

★ RATING: R

★ AGE: 9+

★ RUN TIME: 87 min.

★ AWARDS:
   1987 Academy Award®: Best Writing Adapted Screenplay
      nominee
   1987 Independent Spirit Awards®: Best Feature nominee
   1987 Independent Spirit Awards®: Best Director nominee:
      Rob Reiner

Stand By Me is based on a novella called *The Body* by
Stephen King. The setting for the story, one of King's many
creations outside the horror genre for which he is best known,
was changed from King's usual Maine haunts to a small
Oregon town.

Rated R for extensive profanity, glimpse of a dead body, teenage cigarette smoking; 1986; 87 minutes

A good choice for children 9 or older, especially boys, and parents nostalgic for their lost childhood buddies

S tand By Me is a perfect film for adolescent boys and movie-watching families. Therefore, it's a shame that it was slapped with the dreaded R rating.

This glorious Rob Reiner movie about four boys trekking through rural Oregon is a superb example of how badly the ratings system can serve the art of film. *Stand By Me* qualified for its R on profanity alone, the kind of experimental, don't-really-mean-it swearing that all teenage boys do behind their parents' backs. Throw in just a few F-bombs and you get the R, instead of a PG-13 that would have allowed packs of tweens to see this poignant coming-of-age film on their own.

The 1986 story, based on a Stephen King novella, follows reserved Gordie (Wil Wheaton), crazy-brave Teddy (Corey Feldman), scared Vern (Jerry O'Connell), and leader Chris (River Phoenix) as they search for a rumored dead body miles from their troubled homes. Their mini-odyssey is beset by menacing junkyard owners, abusive bullies, swamps filled with leeches, and, in the most memorable scene, a train that the boys have to outrun over a picturesque trestle.

Their struggle to confront death mirrors the tragedies in their own lives, including Gordie's loss of a beloved older brother and Chris's hatred of his parents. The boys' bond, narrated by Richard Dreyfuss, feels real without coming across as trite, largely because the child actors are so good.

Ignore the profanity. Your kids already know these words. Enjoy with them a great family movie, nominated for a best screenplay Oscar.

Starman

★ GENRE: Comedy / Romance / Sci-Fi & Fantasy

★ RATING: PG

★ AGE: 10+

★ RUN TIME: 115 min.

★ AWARDS:
1985 Academy Award®: Best Actor nominee: Jeff Bridges

The studio that made *Starman*, Columbia Pictures, had another visiting-alien script in hand at the same time. Execs decided not to make both, and they gave up the other script to another studio. The script became *E.T.: The Extra-Terrestrial.*

Rated PG, on the edgier side, for language, some violence and generally mature situations; 1984; 115 minutes

A good choice for children 10 or older, and for parents with a romantic streak

You may be sensing a theme by now: some of the best family movies combine different genres into one film, giving each person on the couch a good reason to keep watching. *Starman* fills that demand, drawing on science fiction, road movies, romantic comedy, and government conspiracies to build a rich entertainment.

Starman showcases the always-likeable Jeff Bridges as an extraterrestrial life form. He acquires the shape of a recently deceased human in order to communicate to Earth his message of peace. The problem for the character played by Karen Allen is that the human form Bridges chooses was her beloved late husband.

She must adjust to this awkward, potentially threatening presence. Then the odd couple must hit the road to avoid capture by military agents who want to study this alien. Their love story grows; it would be absurd if not for the appeal and chemistry of Bridges and Allen together. They eventually make love, and it's clear that she ends the movie pregnant, offering all kinds of potential for family discussions about biblical parallels—Starman descends to Earth to save humankind and leaves a son behind.

What has always stuck with me from *Starman* is the quirky, just-right movement of Bridges as he plays a life form not quite adjusted to gravity. Roger Ebert described it as the actor convincing us "that Jeff Bridges is not inhabited by himself."

The Station Agent

★ **GENRE:** Drama

★ **RATING:** R

★ **AGE:** 12+

★ **RUN TIME:** 90 min.

★ **AWARDS:**

2003 Sundance Film Festival®: Audience Award: Drama
2004 Independent Spirit Awards®: Best Male Lead
nominee: Peter Dinklage

This small-budget indie film was penned by writer-director
Thomas McCarthy specifically for the actors. They shot in a
frenetic twenty days and were so tight on money that
Clarkson's dressing room was formerly a horse trailer.

Rated R, for adult situations, profanity, and some drug content; 2003; 90 minutes

A good choice for children 12 or older, and for parents who love indie films

*M*y parents were less than overwhelmed by *Little Miss Sunshine*, so I had to remind myself why I loved it as more than just another quirky family comedy.

I remembered why, in reading my old review of *The Station Agent* in 2003. The characters in both movies lead interesting, nearly desperate lives, far from the glamour of typical movieland families. The characters' parts are written with a generous, realistic humanity that allows the movies to be life-affirming without trying to tell us exactly how we should live our own lives.

So for your teenagers and mature tweens, try *The Station Agent*, despite its R rating. This quiet film, beloved at the 2003 Denver film festival, introduces us to Fin McBride (Peter Dinklage), a four-foot-five-inch dwarf weary of defending his small stature to a cruel public. He retreats to a decrepit railway station in semirural New Jersey, hoping to be alone for a while. But two more extroverted characters (Bobby Cannavale and Patricia Clarkson) won't leave Fin alone. They have their own problems to solve, and the stoic mystery embodied by Fin draws them out of their isolation.

Like *Little Miss Sunshine*, *The Station Agent* can be a good movie to watch for teenagers starting to feel the pall of alienation. It demonstrates—without preaching—that friendship, progress, and satisfaction can take many forms. Not everybody has to be the quarterback, cheerleader, or captain of the debate team.

Superman

★ GENRE: Action & Adventure

★ RATING: PG

★ AGE: 5+

★ RUN TIME: 150 min.

★ AWARDS:
1979 Academy Award®: Best Film Editing nominee
1979 Academy Award®: Best Sound nominee
1979 Academy Award®: Best Music Score nominee
1979 BAFTA®: Best Supporting Actor nominee:
Gene Hackman

Christopher Reeve was a little-known actor first hired to help feed other Superman actors their lines. He refused to wear a fake-muscle suit and bulked up for the Man of Steel role under the training of David Prowse, who himself went on to be the big body for Darth Vader in *Star Wars.*

Rated PG for mild, cartoonish violence; 1978; 150 minutes

A good choice for children 5 or older, and adults who like to see Hollywood having a good time making a movie

If you spent 148 long minutes with *Superman Returns* in 2006 and wondered why no one in the film seemed to be having a good time, then go back to the super original for movie magic.

Richard Donner's 1978 revival of *Superman* on the big screen was moviemaking now sadly out of style, depicting larger-than-life actors enjoying themselves immensely and bringing the audience along with them almost in spite of a forgettable script.

Picture Christopher Reeve as the definitive man of steel, with a grin somehow innocent and sly at the same time. He enjoyed flying, for crying out loud, and picking up heavy objects to save people sure beat digging ditches for a living. Think of Margot Kidder before she went a bit nutty, playing the pretty-and-difficult love interest with pluck and charm. Kidder and Reeve had a chemistry you can't quite explain by rational career analysis. And then, of course, there is Gene Hackman, chewing up scenery and having a grand old time as Lex Luthor. Hackman loves the movies so much that he appears in half a dozen a year—or so it seems. He's everywhere, yet he never just mails in a role. He made Lex into the funniest guy at the party, even if he was a complete jerk.

Nowadays the style in superhero movies is to explore "the dark, artistic side" and make sure no one enjoys his or her godlike powers. Hey, movies based on comic books aren't meant to taste like medicine. Give me *Superman*, or take a flying leap.

The Sword in the Stone

★ GENRE: Animation

★ RATING: G

★ AGE: 5+

★ RUN TIME: 79 min.

★ AWARDS:
1964 Academy Award®: Best Music Score nominee

This was the first full Disney animated feature using only one director (Wolfgang Reitherman), instead of the team approach used in earlier Disney films.

Rated G; 1963; 79 minutes

A good choice for children 5 and older

Yet another wave of wisecracking cartoon animals in the summer of 2006 sent us in search of more interesting animation ideas from years ago. Far too many mediocre, allegedly hip cartoons were released—*Open Season, The Wild,* and *Barnyard,* to name just a few—and the more we dug for better material, the worse that batch looked.

The Sword in the Stone, for example, dates to 1963 but is ready and waiting to amuse. This gentle take on the King Arthur legend forgoes swordfights and castle sieges for a plot better described as a series of silly interludes.

Young Wart, as the adopted boy Arthur is known by his blustery foster father, scrubs dishes for his family and dreams of better things (*Cinderfella,* anyone?). On a trip through the woods he bumps into Merlin, who has long been expecting him, since Merlin can see into the future. Merlin knows it will be a boy who finally plucks the power-conferring sword from a boulder in distant London.

The best part of the movie is a dueling-wizard battle that puts anything in the *Harry Potter* series to shame. Merlin and Madame Mim turn each other into a hilarious succession of slithering creatures, trying to get the upper wand in a sorcerer's battle for the ages.

Credit-watchers will notice the name of Bill Peet as the screenwriter. Peet had a long and varied career with Disney, and he also penned a terrific series of children's books, including the classic *Farewell to Shady Glade.*

Time Bandits

★ GENRE: Family Life / Sci-Fi & Fantasy

★ RATING: PG

★ AGE: 7+

★ RUN TIME: 110 min.

Terry Gilliam was the only member of Monty Python who was born in America. He finally gave up his U.S. citizenship in 2006, denouncing the Iraq war, after a lifetime of preferring the British sensibility.

Rated PG, for mild language and cartoonish violence; 1981; 110 minutes

A good choice for kids 7 or older looking to explore a rebellious streak, and for parents who love anything Monty Python

Nobody blows bad parents into satisfying little bits better than the Brits, and Terry Gilliam's wildly imaginative *Time Bandits* proudly joined the tradition in 1981.

Young Kevin's nasty mum and dad tell him to shut up so they can watch the telly, but Kevin knows there are more interesting things going on in the world. At night, horsemen crash through his wardrobe into his bedroom, and then a band of larcenous dwarves appears in Kevin's closet. They possess a star map of all the time holes in the universe, and they intend to exploit them to get rich, by looting every age from the Greeks to Robin Hood.

Gilliam adds a level of complication both silly and deep. The Supreme Being wants the map back so it won't fall into the hands of the Source of All Evil. With the dwarves as both instigators and pawns, the battle for control rages across time and space.

Gilliam is the Python who created the bizarrely comic animation interludes between sketches of the revered British comedy show *Monty Python's Flying Circus*. As with later movies in what some see as a trilogy, *Brazil* and *The Adventures of Baron Munchausen*, Gilliam crams *Time Bandits* with elaborate costuming, complex set designs, and every possible gadget. He seems to know that visual chaos is a natural part of viewing the world through a child's eyes.

Time Bandits is the movie for kids and their parents who love Roald Dahl's approach to family life. Adults can be mean, spiteful, and downright intolerable in this fantasyland, and sometimes the bright kids have to run away from mum and dad if they ever hope to enjoy life. Most kids will never need this kind of rebellion, of course, but it's reassuring to children from all families to see that every adolescent is misunderstood at some crucial point in life.

Touching the Void

★ GENRE: Action & Adventure / Documentary / Sports

★ RATING: R

★ AGE: 10+

★ RUN TIME: 106

★ AWARDS: 2004 BAFTA: Best British Film Award

Simon Yates faced biting criticism in the climbing community for his decisions in the movie. But Joe Simpson has always stood by his partner, saying he would have done the same thing and that cutting the rope was the only sane action for a good climber to take.

Rated R for profanity and life-threatening situations; 2003; 106 minutes

A good choice for children over 10 and parents in search of a good adventure—or a discussion about survival and loyalty

Parents largely avoid showing their children documentaries, but they should look around for the right ones to try. A ripping tale from reality can be riveting and uplifting entertainment, and some of the most intriguing family-friendly movies in recent years have come from documentary directors.

Adventure climbers Joe Simpson and Simon Yates dangle as far as anyone can get from the "Hollywood idea of death" in the exhausting docudrama *Touching the Void*. They were climbing an unconquered Andean peak in 1985 when Simpson slid, shattering his leg. A blizzard bore down on the pair. By rights, Yates should have abandoned Simpson to save himself, yet he tried to save his partner by lowering Simpson down the peak on a rope.

A mistake left Simpson hanging in thin air, about to pull Yates off the mountain. Yates cut the rope. Simpson fell hundreds of feet into a crevasse. Yates left him for dead, but Simpson managed to crawl back to base camp in one of the most grueling journeys ever recounted.

Touching the Void tells their story through interviews and impeccable re-creations, producing one jaw-dropping moment after another. Your children may recalibrate their concept of the impossible after sitting through this stunner.

I rarely recommend R-rated movies as family films, but *Void* earns the designation only because of some perfectly understandable profanity. (There are also some harrowing debates about tempting fate.) Most parents who contact us say profanity isn't a problem, since their children know not to use the words.

If you want to learn more about Simpson's views on life, death, and Hollywood, read my 2004 interview with the climber at www.bestfamily films.blogspot.com.

48

Toy Story

★ GENRE: Animation

★ RATING: G

★ AGE: All

★ RUN TIME: 81 min.

★ AWARDS:
   1996 Academy AWARDS: Special Achievement Award:
   John Lasseter

Toy Story was a huge hit. So was its soundtrack, with Randy Newman supplying the endlessly catchy pop tune "You've Got a Friend in Me." The song landed Newman an Oscar nomination, as did the entire score of *Toy Story*.

Rated G, for all audiences; 1995; 81 minutes

A good choice for everyone in the family

*T*oy Story was the first full-length children's feature made entirely with computer-generated animation, and it won a special Oscar for that distinction when it was released in 1995. But the movie is a milestone in modern animation for a much more simple reason: It has a great plot, based on an ingenious, break-the-mindset high concept.

The hit movie set a high bar for the new technology. In the decade and a half since, very few computer animations have come close to *Toy Story's* originality and execution, with the possible exception of *Finding Nemo.*

Toy Story's creators, led by John Lasseter, who has now gone on to lead the merged Disney-Pixar animation studio, knew they still had limitations in computer-generated art. Microchips had trouble, for example, recreating an accurate imitation of human walking or facial features. They had already done a short about a toy come to life, and they knew that computers worked fine when viewers didn't have preconceived notions of how a toy should move. Extending the short to a full-length movie was the next logical step.

And what a story they found, in a team-written script eventually nominated for an Oscar for best original screenplay! The idea is this: Children's toys are alive, and they have a strict set of rules to follow, just as the machines in Isaac Asimov's *I, Robot* do. They are loyal to their owners, they must play dead when humans are in the room, and their owners have a responsibility to treat them decently.

Woody the talking cowboy, voiced by Tom Hanks, is top toy in Andy's house. But Buzz Lightyear (Tim Allen) is the favorite new birthday toy, supplanting Woody and leading to the kidnapping of Buzz by the nasty boy across the street. Woody leads his toy colleagues in a rescue mission, punctuated by a wildly inventive chase scene with a moving van and a rocket-propelled car.

As *The Lion King* did before it, *Toy Story* revived the art of children's animation and ushered in a set of smart movies that entertained children and their parents. It's a landmark movie, and doesn't get old with frequent repetition.

The Truman Show

★ **GENRE:** Comedy

★ **RATING:** PG

★ **AGE:** 9+

★ **RUN TIME:** 102 min.

★ **AWARDS:**

1999 Academy Award®: Best Writing Original Screenplay nominee

1999 Academy Award®: Best Supporting Actor nominee: Ed Harris

1999 Academy Award®: Best Director nominee: Peter Weir

1999 BAFTA®: Best Direction: Peter Weir

1999 BAFTA®: Best Film nominee

1999 BAFTA®: Best Supporting Actor nominee: Ed Harris

Rated PG for adult situations, adult humor; 1998; 102 minutes

A good choice for children 9 or older, and for all parents

If you want a meaty, comment-provoking movie for family night that will engage your tweens and teenagers, you'll find nothing better than *The Truman Show*. The 1998 masterpiece from versatile Australian director Peter Weir predicted our current preoccupation with reality TV, portraying the struggle of a man born to live his entire life on camera.

Jim Carrey, in the best work he has ever done, plays Truman, adopted by a megalomaniacal TV producer (Ed Harris) and raised in a fake village that is actually an enormous TV set. Americans watch Truman's 24-hour show—sleeping and all—in record numbers, but Truman is oblivious. He thinks his perfect wife and his tranquil town are for real.

Truman may be naive, but he's not stupid. He starts noticing oddities in his routine and becomes suspicious. The unraveling of Truman's life and his fight to become his own man free of cameras give *The Truman Show* an unforgettable plot. Next time your kids take a spontaneous picture or movie with their cell-phone cameras, they'll remember this film.

The Truman Show received Oscar nominations for screenplay and direction, but a rich year for movies kept it from a nod for best picture.

The outdoor shots for the fictional Seahaven were filmed in the planned community of Seaside on Florida's panhandle. The idea of a walkable, old-fashioned community with a town square is now the hottest suburban planning concept in America.

What's Eating Gilbert Grape

★ GENRE: Drama / Growing Pains / Family Life

★ RATING: PG-13

★ AGE: 10+

★ RUN TIME: 118 min.

★ AWARDS:
1994 Academy Award®: Best Supporting Actor nominee:
Leonardo DiCaprio

His role as Arnie Grape earned Leonardo DiCaprio his first
Oscar nomination for supporting actor when he was only
nineteen. DiCaprio has since become one of the biggest male
stars on the planet, with two more best-actor Oscar nominations and the lead of the highest-grossing box office movie of
all time, *Titanic.*

Rated PG-13, for mild language, suggestive sexual situations; 1993; 118 minutes

A good choice for children 10 or older, and anyone in the family who struggles with the issues of responsibility vs. freedom

*I*t takes an extremely humane and observant writer and a skilled, thoughtful director to make a movie pitched perfectly for both restless adolescents and their understanding parents.

What's Eating Gilbert Grape is simply a great movie, regardless of genre. No need to pigeonhole it as a family film: it speaks to everyone, with emotion, realism, and a wonderful cast to flesh out the story.

The movie stars Johnny Depp as a small-town eldest son frustrated by the responsibilities of an overweight, housebound mother, a developmentally disabled brother, and a dead-end job in a Main Street grocery store recently bypassed by a discount warehouse on the highway. Gilbert is dying inside for a little freedom, but he's too good a person to shirk his needy brother and his struggling family.

A young Leonardo DiCaprio steals the show as disabled Arnie, remarkably recreating the vocal and emotional tics of a "touched" youth without demeaning the role or himself through caricature.

With supporting efforts by Juliette Lewis, John C. Reilly, Crispin Glover, and Mary Steenburgen, the pressure is off heartthrob Depp. He responds with one of his best performances, striving to be decent while finding his true self.

Lasse Hallström, whom we praised earlier for *My Life as a Dog* and other fine films, directed the movie from a script by Peter Hedges. Hedges also wrote *About a Boy,* one of the most poignant comedies of the past decade, so everything about *What's Eating Gilbert Grape* boasts a fine pedigree.

The sexual content that earned the movie a PG-13 rating, by the way, involves two suggestive but certainly not shocking scenes where the elder Steenburgen tries to seduce Depp.

Young Frankenstein

★ GENRE: Classics / Comedy

★ RATING: PG

★ AGE: 9+

★ RUN TIME: 108 min.

★ AWARDS:
1975 Academy Award®: Best Sound nominee
1975 Academy Award®: Best Writing Adapted Screenplay
   nominee
AFI®: Top 100 Laughs

Universal was (and still is, to a great extent) the "monster" studio—the original home of the great Frankenstein, Dracula, and Wolf Man classics. Mel Brooks used some of the original Frankenstein movie lab equipment, circa 1930s, in his lab scenes for the modern spoof.

Rated PG for risqué subject matter; 1974; 108 minutes

A good choice for children 9 or older, with parents who can explain some of the humor

Young Frankenstein should test current social theories that in our world of snark and irony, children understand satire and parody much earlier than they used to.

And if not, you as the parent still win, because *Young Frankenstein* is one of the funniest American comedies ever made. Who cares if the kids love it? You'll nearly choke laughing.

This pick is in part to honor the recent passing of Peter Boyle, who made his first big comic turn as the tuxedo-wearing monster for Mel Brooks's hit 1974 parody. The family will recognize him from *Everybody Loves Raymond* reruns, but Boyle's best lifetime work was his inspired Frankenstein turn opposite Gene Wilder.

The film has too many great set pieces to list in full. Some are these:

"What knockers!"

"What was the name on the brain you got me, Igor?" "Abby, sir." "Abby what?" "Abby-normal, sir."

"You know, I'm a rather brilliant surgeon. Perhaps I can help you with that hump." "What hump?"

And, of course, there's the "Puttin' On the Ritz" scene, Boyle's tour de force. Brooks spoofs so many Universal Pictures monster classics and his own vaudeville routines that there's barely time to catch a breath. The movie is generous with its female comics too, including a luminously giddy Teri Garr and the acidic Madeline Kahn.

If your kids enjoy this one, they're ready for thicker satirical fare: *Monty Python's Life of Brian* or *The Holy Grail* should be next in your queue.

Christmas Movies

We can't ever pick just one Christmas-themed movie to watch. And my kids have already sat through a mandatory viewing of *It's a Wonderful Life*. (Before: "Ew! It's black and white." After: "That was pretty good.")

So here we offer a small handful of other movies to try with the kids, starting with the Bing Crosby–Ingrid Bergman classic *The Bells of St. Mary's*. Nominated for nine Academy Awards in 1945, this sentimental favorite tells various tales of Father O'Malley and Sister Benedict doing good deeds at their school and in their community. The schoolchildren's version of a nativity play includes a chorus of "Happy Birthday" for the babe in the manger.

Bob Clark's 1983 film *A Christmas Story* has become a perennial favorite among baby boomers and their kids because of its frank message that most families are far from perfect, and that childhood can be a real pain in the mistletoe. The other part of the message, of course, is that despite these truths, you and Ralphie can have a good time anyway.

You've seen *Sleepless in Seattle*, most likely, but do you remember that it all starts on Christmas Eve? That's when lonely Jonah calls a radio talk show seeking a mate for his lonely, widower father (Tom Hanks). The call sets in motion a romance with the beatifically beautiful Meg Ryan. Triple hankies all around, but there is enough real boy in Jonah (Ross Malinger) to please the tough guys in your family.